YOU
SHALL
RECOVER
ALL

YOU SHALL RECOVER ALL

JOHN ECKHARDT

Most Charisma Media products are available at special quantity discounts for bulk purchase for sales promotions, premiums, fundraising, and educational needs. For details, call us at (407) 333-0600 or visit our website at www.charismamedia.com.

You Shall Recover All by John Eckhardt
Published by Charisma House, an imprint of Charisma Media
600 Rinehart Road, Lake Mary, Florida 32746

This book or parts thereof may not be reproduced in any form, stored in a retrieval system, or transmitted in any form by any means—electronic, mechanical, photocopy, recording, or otherwise—without prior written permission of the publisher, except as provided by United States of America copyright law.

Unless otherwise noted, all Scripture quotations are from the King James Version of the Bible.

Scripture quotations marked AMP are from the Amplified® Bible (AMP), Copyright © 2015 by The Lockman Foundation. Used by permission. www.Lockman.org.

Scripture quotations marked AMPC are from the Amplified® Bible (AMPC), Copyright © 1954, 1958, 1962, 1964, 1965, 1987 by The Lockman Foundation. Used by permission. www.Lockman.org.

Scripture quotations marked ASV are from the American Standard Bible.

Scripture quotations from the Common English Bible are copyright © 2010. All rights reserved.

Scripture quotations marked CEV are from the Contemporary English Version, copyright © 1995 by the American Bible Society. Used by permission.

Scripture quotations marked CSB have been taken from the Christian Standard Bible®, Copyright © 2017 by Holman Bible Publishers. Used by permission. Christian Standard Bible® and CSB® are federally registered trademarks of Holman Bible Publishers.

Scripture quotations marked ERV are from the Easy-to Read Version, copyright © 2006 by Bible League International.

Scripture quotations marked GNT are from the Good News Translation in Today's English Version—Second Edition. Copyright © 1992 by American Bible Society. Used by permission.

Scripture quotations marked GW are taken from GOD'S WORD®, © 1995 God's Word to the Nations. Used by permission of Baker Publishing Group.

Scripture quotations marked ICB are taken from the International Children's Bible®, copyright ©1986, 1988, 1999, 2015 by Tommy Nelson. Used by permission.

Scripture quotations marked MSG are from *The Message: The Bible in Contemporary English*, copyright © 1993, 1994, 1995, 1996, 2000, 2001, 2002. Used by permission of NavPress Publishing Group.

Scripture quotations marked NET are from the NET Bible® copyright ©1996-2016 by Biblical Studies Press, L.L.C. http://netbible.com. All rights reserved.

Scripture quotations marked NIRV are taken from the Holy Bible, New International Reader's Version®, NIrV® Copyright © 1995, 1996, 1998, 2014 by Biblica, Inc.® Used by permission of Zondervan. All rights reserved worldwide. www.zondervan.com. The "NIrV" and "New International Reader's Version" are trademarks registered in the United States Patent and Trademark Office by Biblica, Inc.®

Scripture quotations marked NIV are taken from the Holy Bible, New International Version®, NIV®. Copyright © 1973, 1978, 1984, 2011 by Biblica, Inc.® Used by permission of Zondervan. All rights reserved worldwide. www.zondervan.com. The "NIV" and "New International Version" are trademarks registered in the United States Patent and Trademark Office by Biblica, Inc.®

Scripture quotations marked NKJV are taken from the New King James Version®. Copyright © 1982 by Thomas Nelson. Used by permission. All rights reserved.

Scripture quotations marked NLT are from the Holy Bible, New Living Translation, copyright © 1996, 2004, 2007. Used by permission of Tyndale House Publishers, Inc., Wheaton, IL 60189. All rights reserved.

Scripture quotations from The Passion Translation® are copyright © 2017, 2018 by Passion & Fire Ministries, Inc. Used by permission. All rights reserved. ThePassionTranslation.com.

Scripture quotations marked WYC are from the Wycliffe Bible, Copyright © 2001 by Terence P. Noble.

Copyright © 2022 by John Eckhardt
All rights reserved

Visit the author's website at www.johneckhardt.global.

Cataloging-in-Publication Data is on file with the Library of Congress.
International Standard Book Number: 978-1-63641-026-5
E-book ISBN: 978-1-63641-027-2

While the author has made every effort to provide accurate internet addresses at the time of publication, neither the publisher nor the author assumes any responsibility for errors or for changes that occur after publication. Further, the publisher does not have any control over and does not assume any responsibility for author or third-party websites or their content.

22 23 24 25 26 — 9 8 7 6 5 4 3 2 1
Printed in the United States of America

CONTENTS

Chapter 1: The Prelude to Greatness   1

Chapter 2: God Is Your Hope   23

Chapter 3: The World As You've Known It Has Ended   41

Chapter 4: Prospering in the Day of Famine   57

Chapter 5: From Least to Greatest   71

Chapter 6: Let Your Heart Be Enlarged   91

Chapter 7: Restoring Honor   105

Chapter 8: Goodness and Glory   127

Chapter 9: Hope Against Hope   143

Chapter 10: Get Your Edge Back   161

Chapter 11: Keep Dreaming   183

Notes   195

CHAPTER 1

THE PRELUDE TO GREATNESS

You shall increase my greatness, and comfort me on every side.
—Psalm 71:21, NKJV

THERE ARE VERY unusual seasons in life—peculiar times when we collectively experience great difficulty. I am writing this book in early 2021, after a year unlike any I've ever seen before in my lifetime. The world faced a global pandemic and, as a result, a quarantine that kept us home, shut down travel, closed churches, and canceled events. COVID-19 impacted countries' economies. People have lost friends and loved ones to the disease. Others have lost jobs, and businesses have closed. In the United States, all kinds of things have happened in our cities and national government. Social, racial, and political division led to global protests and various kinds of outrage and unrest.

In the midst of all this, the world also weathered natural disasters. Two hurricanes hit just about the same place in Louisiana, causing electrical and food shortages and devastating the region.[1] The state is still recuperating. Can you imagine going through a pandemic, being quarantined and experiencing countless deaths, and then suddenly two deadly storms hit your region? Then, of course, in California, uncontainable fires blazed through the state and its national parks for weeks. In early 2021 Texas experienced unseasonably and deadly freezing weather, fueling major power outages for several days. In Illinois, where I live, we had an unusual storm that produced one-hundred-mile-per-hour winds that snapped trees like twigs. And in East Africa swarms of locusts wiped out acres and acres of crops. It was just a crazy, crazy time underlined by natural disasters, pestilence, and sickness that seemed to linger on, making recovery on any level seem impossible.

Despite what we have seen and gone through—and all the things that have happened in our lives, cities, and the world, in the realms of politics, finance, and the church—God is about to restore everything the locusts have eaten, everything the plague has weakened and rendered lifeless, everything that injustice delayed and hindered. You will recover it all and be released into a realm of greatness you've never experienced before.

As you face uncommon challenges—whether they

are financial, emotional, or relational, whether they involve your ministry or your business—God will not leave you in the trouble unvindicated. God is about to take you to another level despite what you are seeing. As a matter of fact, and even though it's uncomfortable, God often prepares us to move into a new season of expansion when we are in the eye of the storm.

Scripture shows us that one of the prophet's functions is to declare to you the thing God is about to do and to give you some understanding of a situation that might make no sense in the natural. When you look at what's happening in your life during times of difficulty, you might find yourself thinking, "This is crazy. This makes no sense." In connection with things happening nationally and globally, you may be experiencing things you've never experienced before. And if you're not careful, you'll be tempted to believe that your world is coming to an end.

News and media, prophecy teachers, and end-time theorists love this kind of stuff. They'll tell you, "We're living in the last days, and the world is about to end. Hold on and get ready!" They can quickly work you into a panic and a place of fear. So much money is spent, so many platforms are built, and so many bad decisions are made. But we know that perfect love casts out all fear. To cling to that truth, you need a revelation of God's love for you. Because of God's great love, you will not be consumed (Lam. 3:22).

I'm writing this book to let you know that in the

midst of chaos, difficulties, troubles, and pressure, God is setting you up for the greatest breakthrough you've ever known. It may not look like it right now, but what I love about being a prophetic believer is that I can know with certainty that what the enemy means for evil, God can turn around for my good. I can hold on to the promise that God is able to do exceedingly abundantly above all I can ask or think (Eph. 3:20).

Prophetic promises like this give us hope. The word of the Lord comes to give us vision and causes us to see what we cannot see in the natural. In other words, what you see in the natural may look bad, but when the Lord gives you His word, He also gives you the ability to see beyond what is happening in front of you and into what He is doing behind the scenes. His word causes you to dream again, to get a new vision for your future; it sets your focus. Ultimately, a fresh word from the Lord causes you to believe Him again. Despite all the things happening around you—sickness, disease, death, social injustice, political unrest, and economic uncertainty—you will stand assured that God is still on the throne and that He is still about to do something powerful in your life.

EVEN IN THE MIDST OF TROUBLE

Sometimes when the darkness comes, these difficult things are really a prelude to the great things God is about to do. Throughout the Old Testament the prophets—Isaiah, Ezekiel, Daniel, and others—prophesied the Lord's judgment and the consequences to come. But they also prophesied restoration and glory. Isaiah said, "Arise, shine; for thy light is come, and the glory of the Lord is risen upon thee" (Isa. 60:1). Even when "darkness covers the earth," the light of God shall be seen upon you (Isa. 60:2). So even though the Hebrews were in the midst of a bad time, the prophets gave them hope and a prophetic word. Even the Book of Revelation has much to say about judgment. But in the end there's hope because the kingdoms of this world become the kingdoms of our Lord and of His Christ.

So even in the worst of your times, as a prophet of God, I come to prophesy that there is hope, restoration, and victory. When the news delivers a report of yet another disaster or uprising, God is still working to release you into a realm of greatness you've never experienced before. God showed me this as I sought Him for a word to encourage people during what we were facing in 2020 and now in residual trials. He led me to Psalm 71, specifically one verse. Before I share it with you, I want to set up this passage for you.

As you walk with me through these verses, I believe you will find encouragement, the right way to respond, and direction for setting your expectation for what God is preparing to do in your life or ministry—in whatever challenges you're facing.

Don't be confused.

Psalm 71:1 says, "In thee, O Lord, do I put my trust: let me never be put to confusion." This verse is a declaration: "Don't let me be confused about the troubling things that are happening in this season of life." God is not the author of confusion (1 Cor. 14:33). He is the God who makes order out of chaos, peace out of discord. Don't be confused. Though all kinds of things are coming at you and those in the world around you, God is still good. He is still on the throne. He still has a plan for you.

Don't allow the things and the challenges of this season of life to cause you to be confused—confused about God, confused about what God is doing, confused about your own life. One of the worst things that can happen when you go through a season of testing, trial, or attack from the enemy is that you get confused.

Look for a way of escape.

> Deliver me in thy righteousness, and cause me to escape: incline thine ear unto me, and save me.
> —Psalm 71:2

In the midst of all your trouble, God is going to give you a way of escape. You are coming out of the hardship you are going through now. You *will* escape it. Scripture makes that promise.

God has issued a command on your behalf.

> Be thou my strong habitation, whereunto I may continually resort: thou hast given commandment to save me; for thou art my rock and my fortress.
>
> —Psalm 71:3

God has issued a command on your behalf to deliver you and save you out of any situation the enemy has orchestrated. If you've been impacted by the many crises created by the pandemic—or any other thing—God is going to deliver you. He has sent a command—a decree from heaven over your life. And when God commands a thing, it shall happen.

There is deliverance for you.

> Deliver me, O my God, out of the hand of the wicked, out of the hand of the unrighteous and cruel man.
>
> —Psalm 71:4

The psalmist is in a situation where he needs deliverance. He's facing unrighteous and cruel men and needs God's help. The situation doesn't look good, but he begins to call on the name of the Lord. He cries out for deliverance. And just as there was deliverance for David, in the midst of all you are dealing with, there is deliverance for you too. Say it aloud with me right here: "Lord, deliver me."

Oh yes, there is deliverance for God's people, for the saints of God, for the church of the living God, and for *you*.

Always hope.

> For thou art my hope, O Lord God: thou art my trust from my youth.
>
> —Psalm 71:5

When we're walking through the storm, it can be hard to live with hope. In our minds we can know that there is hope in God, but getting that knowledge from our heads to our hearts is not always easy.

I talk to a lot of people who are losing hope right now after all we've been through. They can't find a job. They're hurting emotionally. Their child is depressed. Cancer has struck. Whatever it is, I'm sure you know people who are giving up. They're throwing in the towel. Maybe that's you or your spouse. One of the most beautiful things about serving God is that we can always walk with hope. We can always hope for the best because He promises that the best is yet to come and that the latter days will be better than the former (Hag. 2:9). We can always hope for a good future because He promises that a good and hopeful future is in His plan for our lives (Jer. 29:11). We can believe that things will change and improve because He promises to make roads in the wilderness and rivers in the desert (Isa. 43:19).

When you think about it, living with hope in Christ is what being a believer actually is. It is the basis of our faith—the substance of things *hoped* for and assurance of things unseen (Heb. 11:1). Despite what we see today, we can have hope for America, hope for the world, hope for the nations, and hope for our families and children.

Praise God continually.

> By thee have I been holden up from the womb: thou art he that took me out of my mother's bowels: my praise shall be continually of thee.
> —Psalm 71:6

I love this verse because it tells me that wherever I am in my life, whatever I'm walking through, God has taken care of me all my life, back to my mother's womb. This is not the first time you've faced a crisis or a difficult situation. While this particular season may be unusually hard, we've all gone through storms before. The good news is that if God brought you out then, He will bring you out now.

You are a sign and a wonder.

> I am as a wonder unto many; but thou art my strong refuge.
> —Psalm 71:7

Of all the things you've been through and all the challenges you've overcome, you have a testimony. You are a sign and a wonder. You are a sign of God's grace, power, and mercy. It's a true wonder you're still here. It's a wonder you're still praising God. It's a wonder you haven't given up and thrown in the towel. God is living in you.

God is still with you.

> Let my mouth be filled with thy praise and with thy honour all the day. Cast me not off in the time of old age; forsake me not when my strength faileth. For mine enemies speak against me; and they that lay wait for my soul take counsel together.
> —Psalm 71:8–10

Because God is living in you, He's with you. I know that sounds simple, but I don't think we really get it. The enemy makes people think they're in so much trouble that they believe God has forsaken them. Listen, God has not forsaken the earth. God has not forsaken the church. He has not forsaken you. And God has not forsaken America or any other nation on the earth. God has not forsaken us during this health crisis, political unrest, social injustice, or global pandemic. God is still with us. He is still on our side. He will still deliver and heal you. He tells us to look and says, "See, I am doing a new thing!" (Isa. 43:19, NIV).

No matter what the enemy says or how you might feel, the odds are not against you. God is on your side.

God is your strength.

> O God, be not far from me: O my God, make haste for my help. Let them be confounded and consumed that are adversaries to my soul; let them be covered with reproach and dishonour that seek my hurt. But I will hope continually, and will yet praise thee more and more. My mouth shall shew forth thy righteousness and thy salvation all the day; for I know not the numbers thereof. I will go in the strength of the Lord God: I will make mention of thy righteousness, even of thine only.
>
> —Psalm 71:12–16

Jesus didn't mince words when He told His disciples, "In this world you will have trouble" (John 16:33, NIV). God knows we need His strength when "trouble" comes and threatens us. And He willingly gives it. Let me be clear. It is *His* strength—not your own—that you gain. Say this aloud with me now: "The Lord is the strength of my life."

You will not die.

> Your righteousness, O God, is very high, You who have done great things; O God, who is like You? You, who have shown me great and severe

troubles, shall revive me again, and bring me up again from the depths of the earth.
—Psalm 71:19–20, nkjv

Life can get hard; the challenges can feel so overwhelming. Grief, hurt, loss, disappointment, betrayal, letdown, abandonment, abuse, heartbreak, and injustice are some of the most painful realities of this life. They can be spiritually, emotionally, and mentally traumatizing. We can feel pain so intensely that we think we might die.

Have you ever felt this way? The psalmist of Psalm 71 did, and this is what I want you to see as I walk you through these verses. You are not the first to go through hardship, and you will not be the last. But through it all, God is your helper, provider, Comforter, and defender. This psalmist writes from a place of familiarity with seasons of extreme hardship and difficulty. In the midst of all he's going through, he says something so amazing.

The verses above (19–20) essentially say, "Lord, I am experiencing some things I've never experienced before—great and severe troubles. But I'm not going to die, because You're going to quicken me. You're going to give me life."

Agree with me and say, "I'm not about to die." Say, "I will not die; I will live and declare the works of the Lord."

Earlier I told you I wanted to walk with you through

this passage to get to one specific verse. Let's go there now.

You will end up greater than you were before.

> You shall increase my greatness, and comfort me on every side.
> —Psalm 71:21, NKJV

This particular verse is what I wanted you to see and really let sink in. The psalmist tells us that God is going to do something in your life in the midst of trouble. Out of all of this—a global pandemic, political division, racial injustice, financial trouble, disruption of all kinds, fear, insecurity, relationship breakdowns, grief, and any other trouble you may be going through—you will end up greater than you were before. In other words all the trouble, all the tests, all the things that come against you—things you may have thought would diminish you—they're really the things God is using to prepare you for something greater. God is preparing you for greatness.

I love what the psalmist is saying: in the midst of all that is happening, I need salvation, I need deliverance, I need a hiding place, and I need comfort. But also in the midst of this, I believe God is saying, "When this is all over, let your declaration be, 'Lord, You will increase my greatness.'" Let your faith take hold of this thought for a moment.

God is saying, "You are already great because you

are Mine—because I dwell within you—but I'm going to make you greater." There's another level of greatness coming. We don't really talk about the subject of greatness or hear it talked about in the church because many people don't believe we can have greatness in our own lives. But God did not call you to be average, below average, or mediocre. Scripture says you have been called to greatness in Christ.

I want you to embrace this and begin to confess, "Lord, You will increase my greatness." As you do, your mind will begin to fall in line with God's promise and you'll begin to believe and behave as someone who knows God has a greater place for you. The enemy will try to put a limit on how high you can fly. He will tell you, "You've gone as far as you can go." But God is saying, "There's a greater place I have for you. There's a greater position I have for you. There's greater influence I have for you. There's greater wealth and finances I have for you. There's greater power I have for you. I have a greater platform for you, greater doors. I want to increase your greatness now."

Although the Bible doesn't attribute Psalm 71 to David, it's likely that David did write this psalm. And at the time of its writing, he would have already been a great king. Yet he was still navigating so many trials and tests with his children. We know everything David went through with Saul and all that he walked through with his son Absalom. But if you think about it, on the other side of every trial David faced, God was there, taking him to another level. This is what God wants to do for you.

THE PRELUDE TO GREATNESS

Even if you're living in one of the darkest and most difficult, seemingly hopeless times in your life, I want you to begin to see God's perspective. I want you to confess this prayer that I began to pray some months before I started writing this book:

> *Lord, You are going to increase my greatness. Lord, You are going to increase my influence. Lord, You are going to take me to another level. All the things that have come against me—the things that were designed by the enemy to bring me down and make me low; all the pain and the hurt, the trouble and the tears, and the struggles I've been through—You are going to use as a launching pad to greater greatness. Lord, I didn't understand it at the time, but I hear the word of the Lord now. I see Your hand at work in my life.*

Coming out of your own troubles and expecting God to build and restore you to new levels, you can see why you shouldn't be jealous when you see someone else operating in greatness. Don't hate on them, because you don't know what they went through to get to that place. We often look at the people God promotes and raises up and say things like, "Well, how in the world did *they* get to that place?"

But if you were to sit down and listen to their testimony, you would understand they paid a price to get to that level. I think you'd begin to marvel at how they've trusted God to overcome so much and see how they are indeed a sign and a wonder. Their testimony would probably awe you: "It's a wonder you're still alive. Not only has God preserved you, saved you, and delivered you, but He has brought you to a greater place than you were before."

Never judge a person because of where they are. You may not have been there when they were going through their storm. You weren't there during their seasons of obscurity, testing, and trial.

Look at Joseph—no one but his brothers were there when they threw him in the pit. Only they were there when he was sold to the Ishmaelites. Almost no one was there when he was falsely accused by Potiphar's wife and cast into prison for something he didn't do. It was only when Joseph was promoted to second in command in Egypt and a ring was placed on his finger and a chain around his neck that the masses came to know who Joseph was. All they knew was this new leader's overnight rise to fame.

Never look at a godly person's position and view their rise to greatness negatively. They didn't get to that position overnight. As you hold on to Christ as they did, God will increase your greatness just as He expanded Joseph's territory.

As you read these pages on what we may call "the other side" of the coronavirus pandemic—a season of shutdowns, death, financial troubles, and trials—know that when it looks like things are getting worse and worse, God will bring you into another place of greatness. Get ready to be launched, because what the enemy meant for evil God is turning around for our good.

What you're going through now I call a "prelude" to the greatness God has for you on the other side. So get ready to move to another level. Hold on to the Word of the Lord from Psalm 71:21. David's words give us the confidence that in the midst of all this hell, in the midst of all this trouble, God is about to increase our greatness.

GREATER THAN EVER

The Psalm 71:21 scripture inspired the message of this book, so I want to spend some time breaking down what God taught me as I studied it. Many times the revelation I receive about certain passages in the Bible comes through prayer, of course, but it also comes from word studies in the Greek or Hebrew lexicon, a Bible dictionary, or reading the same passage in different translations. I encourage you to study God's Word in a similar way as well. Diving into the context and word origins will really open up the mysteries of what God is saying to you in certain seasons of life. We're going to do this now with Psalm 71:21. Let's start with the King James Version.

The King James Version translates the verse like this:

> Thou shalt increase my greatness, and comfort me on every side.

It reads like a declaration. But then in some of the other translations the verse reads more like a prayer. For example, the American Standard Version (ASV) says, "Increase thou my greatness, and turn again and comfort me." So here the psalmist is actually *asking* God to increase his greatness. Believers don't usually pray this prayer. You may not have even known you could pray that kind of prayer. But David shows us we can pray and ask God to increase our greatness.

The Amplified Bible translates verse 71 this way: "May You increase my greatness (honor) and turn to comfort me." So here, greatness is also "honor."

The Common English Bible says, "Please increase my honor and comfort me all around." The Contemporary English Version (CEV) says, "You will make me truly great and take my sorrow away," and the English Revised Version (ERV) says, "You will help me do even greater things. You will comfort me again!"

Can you say that aloud with me now? "I'm going to do greater things." When the trouble is all over, the church will still be here, and those who hold on to God will go on to pursue kingdom-building exploits.

Other translations say, "You will make me greater than ever" (GNT, GW). Say this now: "I'll be greater than ever."

"Raise me to a position of great honor," the New English Translation (NET) says.

The New International Revised Version (NIRV) says, "You will honor me more and more."

"Give us even more greatness than before," the psalmist prays in The Passion Translation.

The Wycliffe Bible says, "Thou hast multiplied thy great doing; and thou converted (and thou turned), hast comforted me," indicating that God is about to multiply some great things in your life.

I want you to know that you can claim the promise of Psalm 71:21 and believe that God is about to put new honor on your life. That "disrespect" devil is leaving you. When people don't respect or honor you, don't let you in the room because your name is not on the list, or they sit you in the last row and refuse you a good seat, know that God is about to increase your respect and increase your honor. When greatness comes on you, the people who didn't want to give you any honor and respect will have to reverse their actions. Where you used to be a benchwarmer, only let in the game with twelve seconds left, God is going to raise your level of greatness to the point that you will be able to buy that bench. God is raising your level of greatness and putting you back in the game.

People may have laughed at you and called you a

bum, a benchwarmer, or a scrub. You may have tried to get a shot off only to shoot an air ball. But God is increasing you where it counts and changing your name to something great. The stigma of dishonor is coming off your life. Why? Because you've been through some stuff, and through that season of hardship you held on to God and you didn't give up. You didn't backslide. You kept praising God. You kept praying. You kept worshipping. You kept confessing. You kept serving God. You kept your eyes on Him. During their season of difficulty, other people may have turned and walked away and didn't continue believing God, but you held on. Instead of turning your back on Jesus, you continue to believe Him for deliverance. You have called out to the Lord, and He has heard you and is bringing you out of your situation into something greater. This time of trouble you have been in will not be wasted time.

Declare it like the psalmist did and believe, "Lord, You are going to put something on me that I've never had before. I'm going to another level. The enemy will not laugh at me and mock me. I'll not lose my honor. I will not be put to shame. I will not lose my greatness. Instead, I will have more."

Trust God that He is going to cause you to do greater in your ministry, greater in your career, greater in your business, and greater in your finances. Believe that He is going to cause greater miracles to come your way, greater doors to open, greater platforms to be established, and greater wisdom and grace to be granted. A greater favor is coming on your life than you've ever had before. God's about to open the door, and the door is called Greater.

As I received the word of the Lord for this unique season of difficulty we've faced collectively and individually, I heard Him say to His people, "I'm opening the door of favor, but I'm also opening the door of *greater* favor. There's more favor than you've ever known before. Great resources are about to be put in your hands—great relationships and connections. You're going to meet greater people, and I'm going to take you to greater places. I'm going to give you greater influence. What you thought the locust ate, I am here to restore to you in greater measure than you could ever ask or imagine."

The Lord says, "When this is all over and some people have not made it through, you're going to come out greater. Even though it looks like things began in a bad place, get ready for an upgrade because your end will be better than your beginning. I'm putting a greater crown on your head—greater authority and power. You will have a greater anointing to preach and to prophesy, to cast out devils and heal the sick. I am putting a greater anointing on you to get wealth. I will multiply you and bring you to a greater place of honor, greatness, and favor."

Greatness is something we need to embrace, and you need to believe God for it. Because of the greatness

God gives you on the other side of trouble and hardship, when people look at you, they'll wonder how you got to this place. They may say, "I've known you for many years, and I've never seen you in this kind of place in this kind of position."

You can let them know that you've come out on the other side of testing and trials, and as He promised in Psalm 71, God is increasing your greatness. Often people think they've seen everything there is to see about you. But there are parts of you they've never seen before, and God is going to bring them forth. Through your testimony and witness to the goodness of God, they will know God has done something greater in your life.

CHAPTER 2

GOD IS YOUR HOPE

God is our refuge and strength, a very present help in trouble. Therefore will not we fear, though the earth be removed.

—Psalm 46:1-2

Y᭦ᴏᴜ ᴡɪʟʟ ᴀʟᴡᴀʏs hear me say how important it is for us to understand what is taking place in our lives and in the world around us—and not only for now but also in relationship to what has taken place in the past. This is part of our responsibility as prophetic believers—to be aware of times and seasons. This awareness can help defend your heart against despair. Understanding times and seasons helps you keep perspective when the storms rage, realizing, as Ecclesiastes tells us, there is nothing new under the sun.

The same principles that guided believers for thousands of years in times of trouble will also guide us in whatever season of trouble we're facing today. Remember Jesus' parable about the foolish man and the wise man? The foolish man built his house on sand; the wise man, on rock. (See Matthew 7:24–27.) When we build our spiritual foundation on the truth and revelation of Jesus Christ, we will not fall. He is the true foundation, the Son of the living God. Regardless of what comes, regardless of what goes, His foundation remains steadfast and strong, and we can count on it. We can count on God to be our refuge and strength. Even when our lives are shaking, mountains are trembling, and kingdoms of the world are crashing down, God promises He'll be with us.

GOD IS WITH YOU

Psalm 46 assures us of this promise. For centuries, generation after generation of Christians have found hope and security in these powerful words. Let's read them together.

> God is our refuge and strength, a very present help in trouble. Therefore will not we fear, though the earth be removed, and though the mountains be carried into the midst of the sea; though the waters thereof roar and be troubled, though the mountains shake with the swelling thereof. Selah.
>
> There is a river, the streams whereof shall make glad the city of God, the holy place of the tabernacles of the most High. God is in the midst of her; she shall not be moved: God shall help her, and that right early.

> The heathen raged, the kingdoms were moved: he uttered his voice, the earth melted. The LORD of hosts is with us; the God of Jacob is our refuge. Selah.
>
> Come, behold the works of the LORD, what desolations he hath made in the earth. He maketh wars to cease unto the end of the earth; he breaketh the bow, and cutteth the spear in sunder; he burneth the chariot in the fire. Be still, and know that I am God: I will be exalted among the heathen, I will be exalted in the earth.
>
> The LORD of hosts is with us; the God of Jacob is our refuge. Selah.

The shaking and removing of mountains are symbols of what we're seeing today. Then, in the center of this psalm, the psalmist begins to talk about a river.

> There is a river, the streams whereof shall make glad the city of God, the holy place of the tabernacles of the most High.
>
> —PSALM 46:4

Isn't it interesting that in the midst of all this shaking, of mountains being removed—of fear, trouble, and wars—the psalmist talks about a river? The river of God is one of my favorite subjects. I want you to understand why this river is so important to us today.

The river imagery we read throughout Scripture is a

picture of the moving of the Holy Spirit and the flow of the Spirit of God. Let's look at some examples:

In John 7:38, Jesus used this river imagery when He said, "Out of [your] belly shall flow rivers of living water."

John saw the river in the Book of Revelation, as a river flowing from the throne of God (Rev. 22:1). The river in Zion is also called "the river of God."

In his vision Ezekiel saw a river flowing over all sides of the temple (Ezek. 47:1–3).

So as we see this river appearing in Psalm 46, the psalmist wants us to understand the importance of being Spirit-filled during times of trouble. Being Spirit-filled is not just speaking in tongues, prophesying, and having gifts of the Spirit that manifest in a church service. No. The gifts of the Spirit and the river of God should always flow from your life, especially during times of trouble. We need the Spirit of God. We need the river of God. We need the sustaining flow of the Spirit of God.

BE FILLED AND DO NOT BE AFRAID

In early 2020, I encountered so many people who were afraid. It was as if fear were in the air. People didn't know what to do. They couldn't get a read on what was coming, not only with health-related issues but also economically.

When we read about the rule, reign, and dominion

of God in Psalm 46, we learn that God often establishes His rule, reign, and dominion in the midst of trouble. In fact, before He establishes the rule, reign, dominion, and kingdom of God, God often has to shake old systems. He shakes old government and economic systems—systems of sin. Look at Babylon, Egypt, and Sodom in Scripture. One of the ways God establishes His kingdom in our lives is by removing the old kingdoms. So many times, He does this in seasons of trouble.

As believers filled with the Spirit of God, we can learn to not be afraid in difficult times. We don't need to panic and give up. What God is doing during these times is really the result of the prayers God's people have been praying for many years. We pray for the removal of wickedness, ungodly leadership, injustice, and unrighteousness. And God is answering our prayers and establishing His rule in the midst of the shaking.

If you continue in the Psalms to Psalm 47, the writer begins with, "O clap your hands, all ye people; shout unto God with the voice of triumph" (v. 1). The psalmist then proceeds to write about the rule and reign of God coming. Then in Psalm 48 the subject moves to Zion, the city of God, the mountain of God, the stronghold of God, and the rule and reign of God. These three psalms reveal a powerful progression. Psalm 46 focuses on God removing old kingdoms.

Psalm 47 talks about praising and worshipping God as God's kingdom and rule are established.

> O clap your hands, all ye people; shout unto God with the voice of triumph. For the LORD most high is terrible; he is a great King over all the earth. He shall subdue the people under us, and the nations under our feet. He shall choose our inheritance for us, the excellency of Jacob whom he loved. Selah.
>
> God is gone up with a shout, the LORD with the sound of a trumpet. Sing praises to God, sing praises: sing praises unto our King, sing praises. For God is the King of all the earth: sing ye praises with understanding.
>
> God reigneth over the heathen: God sitteth upon the throne of his holiness. The princes of the people are gathered together, even the people of the God of Abraham: for the shields of the earth belong unto God: he is greatly exalted.
>
> —PSALM 47

Finally, Psalm 48 reveals the establishment of Zion, the city of God, the rule and reign of God, the mountain of God, and the river of God.

> Great is the LORD, and greatly to be praised in the city of our God, in the mountain of his holiness. Beautiful for situation, the joy of the whole earth, is mount Zion, on the sides of the north, the city of the great King. God is known in her palaces for a refuge.

> For, lo, the kings were assembled, they passed by together. They saw it, and so they marvelled; they were troubled, and hasted away. Fear took hold upon them there, and pain, as of a woman in travail. Thou breakest the ships of Tarshish with an east wind. As we have heard, so have we seen in the city of the LORD of hosts, in the city of our God: God will establish it for ever. Selah.
> We have thought of thy lovingkindness, O God, in the midst of thy temple. According to thy name, O God, so is thy praise unto the ends of the earth: thy right hand is full of righteousness. Let mount Zion rejoice, let the daughters of Judah be glad, because of thy judgments.
> Walk about Zion, and go round about her: tell the towers thereof. Mark ye well her bulwarks, consider her palaces; that ye may tell it to the generation following. For this God is our God for ever and ever: he will be our guide even unto death.
>
> —PSALM 48

This river of God flows in the midst of the city, in the midst of Zion, in the midst of the shaking, and in the midst of the mountains being removed. When you're walking through the fire, letting the Spirit of God flow in your life is so critical. That river may flow by way of dreams, visions, prayer, intercession, tongues, interpretation of tongues, words of knowledge, or words of wisdom. This river of God's Spirit brings gladness and the peace of God—the *shalom* of God. It brings the wisdom of God. It brings just what we need.

And this river is all-encompassing—not just for a church service. During the health crisis in 2020 and early 2021, one of the first things Christians couldn't do was gather together in church buildings. And yet the river of God continued to flow. This river of living water (John 7:38) is really the difference between a Spirit-filled believer and those who do not have the Spirit of God. That difference is magnified even more intensely in dark times.

If you don't tap into the Spirit of God or have not received His Spirit, you will find yourself full of fear and panic. You'll be afraid, confused, not knowing what to do. But with the Spirit, you can trust in God for His peace, power, and anointing. You can lean on Him to fill you with His joy and the gladness of God. And you can look to Him for His wisdom. In the midst of this great shaking and trouble God says, "I will be with you." He stays with us through His Holy Spirit. That's how God inhabits and dwells in us. He lives in us through the always-flowing river of His Spirit.

Wherever we worship, whether it's in a church building surrounded by a crowd or in a living room with four family members, we need to pray in tongues, pray with interpretation, prophesy, and flow in words of wisdom. We need to let the peace of God, the glory of God, and the grace of God flow in and through our lives. Let that river flow out of your belly. Don't limit the river to a church service. When we are filled with God's Spirit, we can live in power and not be afraid.

YOU ARE THE MOUNTAIN OF GOD

My guess is you've been told you are a temple of the living God. If you haven't, read 1 Corinthians 3:16. But did you know you are also the city of God and you are Zion? I talk about this identity in my book *I Am Zion*.

Understanding the fullness of Zion teaches us that our identity is in Christ. Zion is also synonymous with the mountain of God, the city of God, the river of God, the dominion of God, the power of God, the fortress of God, the habitation of God, the presence of God, the glory of God, and the wisdom of God. All are in Zion—the place of God's glory, light, excellence, and favor.

Though all the mountains in Psalm 46 are removed and cast into the sea, there is one mountain that stands strong, one mountain that can never be removed. That mountain is Zion because it is God's mountain. It is a place of stability and righteousness, a place that cannot be overthrown. An eternal place. From generation to generation—it is everlasting. It is a place of the rule and reign of God. And that's who you are. That's who I am. We are Zion.

I encourage you to get a revelation of Zion because truly understanding its nature and the identity Zion brings will give you a firm foundation you can boldly stand on when everything around you is falling apart. Like a tree planted by the water, you will not be moved. You can see systems, governments, economies, and health systems falling apart, but because you are the mountain of God and your hope is in Him, you can be secure. Peace, joy, victory, celebration, dancing, rejoicing, glory, anointing, presence, and favor are all yours.

YOU ARE HEALED AND RESTORED

> In the midst of the street of it, and on either side of the river, was there the tree of life, which bare twelve manner of fruits, and yielded her fruit every month: and the leaves of the tree were for the healing of the nations.
> —Revelation 22:2

In addition to being a refuge and a place of God's presence, the river is also a place of healing and restoration. In a vision, John the Baptist saw the river of God flowing, and wherever it went the living water brought healing to the nations. This is exactly what the nations are looking for now. When I wrote this book in 2020, the nations were looking for healing. Since then, many people have been healed. Healing flows through the river. The river flows in Zion. The church is the place of healing, the place of restoration, and the leaves of the tree are for the healing of the nations. This is the kingdom. This is what we are. This is who we are. This is something you can only understand through the Spirit and the Word of God. The more we study this identity, the more we dig it out, the more we confess it, and the more we understand it, the less we will be shaken by what is happening around us and in our lives.

YOU WILL NOT BE MOVED

Be encouraged, because even though the mountains are shaking and you may see trouble on every side, we know God is in the midst of Zion. God is with you. He stands with you. He strengthens you. God is moving, protecting, and covering you. I don't think you can ever read these five verses enough:

> God is our refuge and strength, a very present help in trouble. Therefore will not we fear, though the earth be removed, and though the mountains be carried into the midst of the sea; though the waters thereof roar and be troubled, though the mountains shake with the swelling thereof. Selah.
> There is a river, the streams whereof shall make glad the city of God, the holy place of the tabernacles of the most High. God is in the midst of her; she shall not be moved.
> —PSALM 46:1–5

Declare this now:

- I will not be moved.
- I am Zion.
- I am the mountain of God.
- Even though things around me may shake, I will not be moved.
- God will help me.

Now look again at the next three verses of Psalm 46:

> The heathen raged, the kingdoms were moved: he uttered his voice, the earth melted. The LORD of hosts is with us; the God of Jacob is our refuge. Selah.
> Come, behold the works of the LORD, what desolations he hath made in the earth. He maketh wars to cease unto the end of the earth.
> —PSALM 46:6–9

God is the One who causes all the wars and all the trouble to cease, and He will be with you in whatever situation you're facing. You are in a war with an invisible enemy, but you do not have to be afraid. God is going to cause that fear to cease because His Spirit dwells in you and fills you.

> ...he breaketh the bow, and cutteth the spear in sunder; he burneth the chariot in the fire. Be still, and know that I am God: I will be exalted

among the heathen, I will be exalted in the earth.
—Psalm 46:9–10

Through the trouble and shaking we deal with in our lives both individually and collectively, God will be exalted. His rule, His city, His place—which is within you—will be promoted and lifted up. Scripture tells us that when everything else fails, the kingdom of God continues, from generation to generation.

> The Lord of hosts is with us; the God of Jacob is our refuge. Selah.
> —Psalm 46:11

Psalm 46, Psalm 47, and Psalm 48 reveal God's plan for His church: Out of the shaking, out of the fear, out of the trouble, God protects us and covers us. His river flows. Healing flows. Recovery and restoration flow. God's true reign and majesty will be exalted and established as He removes all the wickedness. God's people will stand, and the river of God will flow from your belly from generation to generation.

BE ENCOURAGED—
BREAKTHROUGH IS HERE

Sometimes we read and study and get hope from passages like these three psalms, but our hearts are still sick because of the delay. Even though we hope in God, our hopes and dreams never seem to come to pass. Delay can bring on disappointment, hopelessness, discouragement, and even depression and sadness. Often the enemy will attempt to block, obstruct, delay, attack, and hinder God's promises from coming to pass.

My mind always goes to Daniel when I think about this. Daniel's prayer was held up for twenty-one days because a supernatural battle was waging in the heavenlies. (See Daniel 10.) The Bible says there was a messenger of Satan, a "demonic prince," who was blocking the answer to Daniel's prayer. But God sent an angel to break through.

By Daniel's testimony we know that there can be demonic interference that holds up the answers we seek from God. And so I want to give you something to hold on to and grasp, despite the enemy's attempt to derail your hope.

Proverbs 13:12 in The Message says, "Unrelenting disappointment leaves you heartsick, but a sudden good break can turn life around." If you're facing disappointment, hopelessness, discouragement, and despair, and it seems like nothing is breaking through, I want you to believe God with me that you will receive a *sudden* breakthrough, a *sudden* miracle.

Many times in life when we're faced with seemingly insurmountable challenges, we are really in need of a miracle. I believe in miracles. I believe God is a miracle-working God. The Bible is full of miracles that came suddenly for people who were in desperate need.

Note again that Proverbs 13:12 says, "Unrelenting

disappointment leaves you heartsick" (MSG). *Unrelenting disappointment.* This disappointment doesn't end; it just goes on and on. You suffer disappointment after disappointment. Look at the second part of the proverb: "But a sudden good break can turn life around" (MSG). Oh, hallelujah!

You may be heartsick reading these words right now. You may be sad, discouraged, and frustrated, even to the point of depression, heaviness, and grief. All you need is a sudden good break. Just one miracle in your finances, your business, your health, your relationship, or your career. One door opening; one relationship connection—you need one miracle to turn around all of that depression, sadness, disappointment, heartsickness, and those years of disappointment.

You've been praying. You've been giving. You've even been fasting. You may be at the point of weeping and crying, yet all the while confessing, decreeing, and believing. Still, it looks like disappointment is your lot in life.

Today I want us to believe God together for a "sudden good break." This can apply to your financial affairs, your business, your career—whether you need a job or a new position. Just one sudden good break. I'm also talking about healing, deliverance, and relationship breakthroughs. I'm talking about salvation for your sons, daughters, loved ones, and family. Maybe you are asking God to do something about your housing situation or transportation.

The old system that benefits only the proud and arrogant and certain people is coming down. The new is coming to those who are faithful and humble, to those who love God and put their trust in Him, to those who depend on God more than man. We don't have to depend on a system to be blessed. We depend on the kingdom, and we depend on God. He is your hope, and He will not disappoint you. Whatever you need, let's believe God for His sudden breakthroughs.

PRAYER FOR SUDDEN BREAKTHROUGH

Jesus, come into my life as the breaker. Lord, I believe that You are the breaker. I believe that You can break through the stronghold—any yoke, any cycle, any season of disappointment—operating in my life. I believe, Lord, You can break any delay, any long time of not seeing breakthroughs and progress.

I thank You, Lord, and I call upon You as my breaker today. Go before me and break through any limitation and any long cycle of illness, poverty, lack, or bad relationships. I pray, Lord, that You would come and give me a sudden good break. Lord, I pray for sudden breakthroughs. I pray for miracle breakthroughs. I decree miracle turnarounds to happen in my life, in the name of Jesus.

I decree that this next season will be a season of turnaround—my turnaround season. Lord, I pray that You would cause me to break through things that have held me back. Lord, come and break through delay, break through denial, break through demonic opposition, break through demonic resistance, break through witchcraft, break through any curses, break through long failure, and break through seasons of unrelenting disappointment.

Let there be breakthrough! Let me see breakthroughs in my finances, in the way I live, in my health, in my relationships, and in my business or ministry. Lord, cause me to see sudden good breaks in my life. Let this season of unrelenting disappointment come to an end.

I decree that I am breaking out of this season of disappointment, discouragement, frustration, failure, lack, sickness, hopelessness, despair, depression, weeping, crying, or loneliness. I declare that I am coming into a new season of divine turnaround—a season of divine breakthrough, of miracles and wealth, of favor and health, of wholeness and healing, and of success, joy, celebration, and the goodness of the Lord. I am walking into good things.

Father, I thank You for giving me hope. Thank You for giving me breakthrough and for being my breaker. In Jesus' name, amen.

CHAPTER 3

THE WORLD AS YOU'VE KNOWN IT HAS ENDED

MAJOR DISRUPTIONS TO the course of your everyday life—whether financial issues; changes to your physical health; the death of a loved one; a sudden change in employment; an unexpected relocation; loss of a close relationship; or threats to your safety due to war, terror, or natural disaster—may cause you to feel like it's all over. Your world is ending, and there's nothing you can do. Nothing will ever be the same again, you may fear. You may feel disoriented, helpless, defenseless, out of control, hopeless, unheard, and invisible.

It's true—these kinds of disruptions do signal the end of a season or an era. They signal the end of something old and the dawn of something new. It's not often that we like or feel as if we can endure changes of this magnitude. We may feel like all is lost and nothing can be salvaged. We may even feel like we will not survive the stress and strain. But I want you to declare with me, "I shall not die, but live, and declare the works of the LORD" (Ps. 118:17). Maybe you only said this in faith. That's OK. Say it again as many times as you need to, getting louder and stronger each time until this truth becomes real to you.

I want you to know that in this dark season, you can count on God. His Word says you will not die (Ps. 118:17, author's paraphrase). In other words, God will quicken you and give you life. The enemy may have sent the situation you are facing to take you out, but God wants to use it to bring in something new and better. His justice and judgment will not let evil prevail. He will vindicate you and make all things new. But first the old ways, mindsets, and systems must go. They served you well for a season. But where God is taking you next requires something different. A shift in priorities is necessary.

Since the pandemic and the racial and political upheaval that marked the start of the 2020 decade, we've been dealing with not only sickness and death related to coronavirus but also issues of injustice and a new way of being the church. After George Floyd's death on May 25, 2020, in Minneapolis, protesting took place around the country and the world. In my city of Chicago we saw businesses looted, peaceful marches, and violent uprising. In many ways we are still living in a divided and polarized culture.

I believe the chaos and unrest (both then and now) can be used for good. Genesis 50:20 is clear: "But as for you, ye thought evil against me; but God meant it unto good." What seemed like chaos can be seen as God turning things, just as He said He would in Psalm 71:21: "Thou hast multiplied thy great doing; and thou converted (and thou turned)" (WYC). What was meant for evil can be turned in our favor and work for our good. Testimony after testimony proves that when God turns His attention to an issue or situation, He brings deliverance, vindication, justice, and restoration for things that have been broken down, desolate, or wrong for so long. Some of us have not only been watching the news and seeing destruction, but we've also experienced this in our own lives. As we believe that God will work through our adversity, we need to be ready to hold on, because deliverance and restoration don't always come in the way we think they will.

Think about how the Jewish people saw Jesus, the fulfillment of all that had been prophesied in the Old Testament. He did not come in military power and strength as an earthly king, as they thought He would. Many didn't even recognize Him as Messiah (and still don't). For some, persecution and oppression increased. But what many did not understand, like many of us today, was that the world was not ending. It was changing. The way things had been going was changing. God's judgment had come to set things right. Things could not remain the way they had once been. Old systems had to come down before the new could be established.

We are in a season much like that both collectively and individually. God wants to shake things up. He wants to recalibrate and realign us with His priorities. How else can He trust us with the great things He is planning to release to us?

You may look at all the chaos and trouble in your life and feel as if God has turned away from you. Let me assure you that He has not. God is turning toward you. He wants to show you what matters most to Him in this hour so that you can be in line with His Spirit—so that when you have recovered all that has been lost, you'll be in a position to keep it. You'll be in a position to carry His light and glory. What happened in the days following a pivotal event in 2020 was the catalyst for the revelation God gave me about why certain things must have cataclysmic endings for glorious beginnings to manifest.

WEIGHTIER MATTERS

The Bible does say there is a time and season for everything. There's a time to speak and a time to refrain from speaking. I believe the time around George Floyd's death was a time for many to speak. And many did. Pastors, politicians, media personalities, actors, and everyday citizens used their platforms, their voices, to speak on injustice, racism, prejudice, hatred, and murder. At the height of the protests, I went live on Facebook and spoke from my heart as many others did. I shared a verse from Matthew 23 the Lord had laid on my heart:

> Woe to you, scribes and Pharisees, hypocrites! For you pay tithe of mint and anise and cummin, and have neglected the weightier matters of the law: justice and mercy and faith. These you ought to have done, without leaving the others undone.
> —MATTHEW 23:23, NKJV

Notice that Jesus referred to some things in the law as weightier or more important, and He called out three things:

1. Judgment or justice
2. Mercy or compassion
3. Faith or faithfulness

These are the weightier things of the law.

When I say the world is changing right before our eyes, it's not an understatement. The ground is shifting beneath us. Some are even prophesying the end of the world. I shared my views about this in the last chapter, but one thing I can agree with is this: as we came out of the shutdown or quarantine because of the coronavirus, the world was not the same. Things have not returned to the way they used to be. The pandemic alone was enough to change the world. But on top of that, and in the same year, the George Floyd video went viral. The world watched as Minnesota police officer Derek Chauvin kneeled on the neck of George Floyd. Despite Floyd's cries, Chauvin did not move and remained there for nearly ten minutes until Floyd's cries were no more.[1] In the same year, nearly three million people worldwide died from coronavirus.[2] The number seems so large, and some may find it impersonal, but you gain a greater perspective of life if your loved one was one of those three million.

It takes a year like 2020 to cause us to realize that sometimes what we choose to argue and fight about are not the weightier matters—like the arguments over if, how, or when we should gather and whether or not to follow social distancing rules or wear masks. We can get involved in all kinds of material pursuits. But what did Jesus say? "What shall a man give in exchange for his soul?" (Mark 8:37).

Your life is the most important gift God has given you. I know we have to work and make money. We want to enjoy life and have good things. I've taught about the good land and the good life. I believe in prosperity and abundance. But sometimes the things we cherish are material things.

Rioting and looting are not good, of course. A community may take years to come back as a result. But the lost goods or property are material things. Some people were more upset about the act of looting than they were about the violent act that fueled the rage.

This is why I believe the Lord led me to Matthew 23:23. Here, Jesus talked about judgment being a weightier matter. The words "weightier matter" tell us that there are some things that are more important to God than others. And sometimes, as Matthew 23:24 says, we can "strain at a gnat, and swallow a camel."

Sometimes we can fight and argue over nonessential matters and miss what God is doing. Sometimes we're not too different from the Pharisees—and Jesus called them hypocrites. He said that they would argue and fight over tithes, but they would ignore judgment, mercy, and faith. He was telling the religious leaders of His day, "You'll go to church. You'll give tithes. You're very legalistic in the small details of the law, but you ignore justice and judgment, mercy and compassion." Understand that He was not telling them not to tithe. He was simply telling them not to be hypocritical. Don't major on the minors and minor on the majors.

Until justice, mercy, and faith are weighed proportionately, people will be angry, outraged, and upset. The plight of the poor and the oppression of minorities in America, as well as in other parts of the world, have been ignored. When we see injustice against people who are powerless by people who are more powerful, that's when we should feel outraged. God certainly does.

TURNING OVER TABLES

God hates injustice. He hates when there's no judgment, mercy, or compassion in the land. He hates when there's no faith or faithfulness. These are the weightier matters of the law, and we should also be concerned about these issues and realize our call to serve Him involves us giving these issues prominence even in how we live our lives.

Just as Jesus turned over tables in the temple, God is turning over what we have come to value. Because we are part of His family, God desires to bless us. But we cannot expect to receive from Him if we do not value what He values. God used the racial, health, and political events of 2020 to show us where we are getting it wrong and to help us come back into covenant with Him on those issues.

For years people have complained about injustice, and in the case of George Floyd and others, police brutality. This was the season in which things came to light in a way they never had before. On April 20, 2021, former Minneapolis police officer Derek Chauvin was found guilty of all charges for the death of George Floyd. At the time this book went to press, the other three officers involved were still awaiting trial. The fact that there was video evidence that led to the results of this case showed us the world is not the same as it was forty or fifty years ago. Now everyone has a phone with a camera. The things we tried to ignore or deny in the past are impossible to ignore today. We're going to have to deal with justice and injustice. God is calling us back to the weightier matters.

A NEW WAY OF THINKING

The pandemic and all the occurrences of 2020 were about transition. The world as we may have known it did come to an end. Not only did we enter a new decade, but we also entered a new world.

We don't live in the same world anymore. If you think about it, the world is always ending. Certain events happen that signal a shift and tell us the old world is ending. If you don't keep up with what God is doing and calling for from one era to the next, you'll be trying to live in the new with an old mentality. If you don't shift and change and walk in the new, you'll be outmoded and outdated. When you see things like this happening, you know that God is saying the old world is ending. The world as you know it is coming to an end. To step over into a new world, you must begin to think differently.

Derek Chauvin put his knee on another man's neck, refusing to realize that the man under his knee was made in the image of God. You are made in the image of God. And so is everyone else in this world. But do we really see and internalize that? If you're honest with yourself, do you sometimes look down on people for their position in society, their age, their gender, or the color of their skin? We need to be careful that we do not begin to dehumanize people and see them as less important than ourselves or others. How we view others has everything to do with how we practice justice, mercy, and faith.

We need to recover the understanding that every person—no matter how they look and no matter their situation—is made in the image of God. And you must love, honor, and respect them. Sometimes we look down on people because we see them as unimportant.

A PRIEST, A LEVITE, AND A SAMARITAN WALK DOWN THE STREET

In Luke 10:25–37 Jesus tells a story about a man who had been robbed and beaten. He was bleeding and dying on a road going from Jerusalem to Jericho. A priest and a Levite walked by him on their way to wherever they were going. (Though Scripture doesn't say this, I like to imagine they were going to church or the synagogue.) Then Jesus says that a Samaritan stopped, put oil and wine in the man's wounds, picked him up, and took him to the city. There, he paid for the injured man to stay in an inn until he was well. Why did the Samaritan do this? Because the man who was dying and bleeding was made in the image of God.

Religion will walk right by you when you're hurting and dying. The priest and Levite were too busy getting to church; they didn't make time to stop. Instead, they stepped over the bloody scene and went on their way.

I think about the response people had during the pandemic about churches being shut down. Some cried loudly about not having a church service during the pandemic, but we didn't hear much from them when it came to the injustice surrounding the loss of George Floyd's life. Based on Matthew 23:23, we can understand that God is saying, "Your church service is not as important as justice, mercy, and faith."

So it was a Samaritan who stopped and cared for the injured man. The Samaritan was someone the priest and the Levite were taught to despise, someone they looked down on. Samaritans were people who weren't even qualified to be in the same house with a Jew.

Sometimes the people we look down on have more compassion and mercy than the ones we look up to. It's true. And this is why I say the world has changed. The weightier matters, the most important things, are not our statuses, our jobs, our cars, our homes, or our successes—and I believe in being blessed. God says the weightier matters are justice, which is judgment; faith, which is faithfulness; and mercy, which is compassion. Those are the weightier matters. They are more important to God than church services, shouting, dancing, and running—and I'm all for shouting and dancing and running. But preachers will spend so much time talking about their right to have a service, of which they've had thousands, yet when it comes to issues of human value and life, you won't hear a peep out of them. They'll be more concerned about religious things, such as whether women can preach, wear pants, or be prophets or apostles.

A WHOLE NEW WORLD

So yes, the old world is ending. We no longer live in the same world we used to live in. I was born in 1957, so I can say I've lived through several world endings. I don't live in the same world I was born into. I live in a different world, and I must be able to change and move in the new things God is calling us to. I need to be able to recognize when things are changing and the world is shifting. When it comes to where God wants to take us, we cannot be outmoded geezers. We cannot be so set in our ways, living in the past and not being able to move in the new. We will get left behind. For God to take us into greater things, our thoughts must be aligned with His thoughts. We must prioritize what He says is important. This season should have shown us this.

Shifts like these are why I love the prophetic, because the prophetic always declares, "Behold, the former things are come to pass, and new things do I declare: before they spring forth I tell you of them" (Isa. 42:9). God is always making things new. He is always doing something new, ending the old and releasing the new. I'm writing this to let you know that even though it looks bad, actually terrible now, the new will be better. And sometimes you have to go through bad things before you walk into the new.

Sometimes injustice, both on the national stage and in our own lives, must come to a head before the shift to justice, mercy, and faith takes hold.

Think about Noah. His world literally came to an end when the rain began to fall. But when he came out of that ark—out of God-ordained quarantine—he and his family had a new start. When God released His Spirit on the day of Pentecost, that was the symbolic release of a new era, a new wind.

In all these examples, God released a new spirit, and that's what He's doing now. God is going to release a new wind, a new spirit, and a new breath upon the church. The church is going to be new. We're not going to do church the same way we've done it in the past, so we'd better get rid of our old models and our old ways of doing church. God forced us to physically shut down church because He said, "You're not going to continue to do it the way you've been doing it. You must do something new, something fresh." We'll have to reach people in a different way and do things differently. Different than one church service after another, conference after conference ad nauseam with the same songs, the same sermons, and the same messages. God is saying, "No more. You'd better wake up and realize you're in a new day. And if you try to live in the new the same way you lived in the old, you'll be outdated, outmoded, and left behind. You'll be a dinosaur. You might as well call your church Jurassic Assembly, because that's what it will be."

We're embarking on not only a new decade but also

a new season. And out of the old comes the new—resurrection comes, Pentecost comes, and the Spirit of God is released. A new people are born who honor what God honors. A new spirit and a new wave come. God always does something new. Get ready for it.

KINGDOM WITHOUT END

Despite all the pain and death, the violence, and the prejudices on this earth, I am not afraid. I am a prophetic man. I understand that times and seasons change. I'm a kingdom man, and what I understand is that even though the world ends, the kingdom has no end. The kingdom continues. Isaiah 9:7 says, "Of the increase of his government and peace there shall be no end, upon the throne of David." God will order righteousness and justice (Ps. 89:14).

When you're in the kingdom, you live in an everlasting, eternal realm. You have eternal life now, and you keep moving in the new. You keep pressing in the new. You know that even though the old is over, God creates a new wineskin. The new things God is doing are going to be better. Revival is coming. Glory is coming. The church is rising; it will not be left behind. As we stay aligned with God, we are not going to be stuck in the old. Some denominations and some groups are going to be Jurassic. They will end. They've been dead for years. Some preachers' messages will become irrelevant and obsolete.

But I'm here to let you know that those who move

in the Spirit; those who live in the kingdom; those who receive the new; those who are prophetic; those who have eyes to see; the pioneers, trailblazers, and pathfinders; those who are sent by God; and those who believe in the new and receive a fresh anointing—they will not be left behind. You can be among that number by making what matters to God your priority, and you will come forth with a greater anointing in the days to come.

THERE WILL BE JUSTICE

I'm encouraged. I believe the best is yet to come. When God removes the old, He raises up something new and something better. When the old ends and the new comes in, there will be more justice. The world won't be perfect overnight, but I'm telling you, a lot of the "old" is coming to an end.

We live in a new day in which certain things will not be tolerated anymore. Police brutality, abuse of power, and oppression of minorities—these things will not be tolerated. People are saying, "We're tired of this. Enough is enough." I believe this is what God is saying too. He wants to see His justice roll down like a river both in the world around you and in your life. He wants to see things made right on your behalf. Whatever is yours that has been blocked, held back, hindered, or locked up—God is releasing His justice, mercy, and faithfulness on your behalf.

A new world was birthed in 2020. I hope you

marked it down—a new decade, new year, and new world. There will be other endings in the days to come. Something else will happen that will change the world. I don't know when it will happen, but it will happen.

Hebrews 8:6 and 13 says, "He is the mediator of a better covenant, which was established upon better promises....In that he saith, a new covenant, he hath made the first old. Now that which decayeth and waxeth old is ready to vanish away."

God gave a better covenant, a new covenant, and a better priesthood in the order of Melchizedek. The promise of God was better. Jesus was better than Moses. The new is always better than the old.

Those who have been oppressed, beaten down, ignored, overlooked, and rejected are going to come forth. They will rise. Those who have been proud, arrogant, lifted up, abusive, and controlling will come down. God is going to bring some down, and He's going to promote others. He is going to humble the proud and exalt the humble. He always does that.

The old system that benefits only the proud and arrogant, and certain people, is coming down. This is justice. The new is coming to those who are faithful and humble, to those who love God and put their trust in Him, and to those who depend on God more than man. We don't have to depend on a system to be blessed. We depend on the kingdom, and we depend on God. His justice is coming.

CHAPTER 4

PROSPERING IN THE DAY OF FAMINE

They shall not be ashamed in the evil time: and in the days of famine they shall be satisfied.
—Psalm 37:19

I WANT TO CONTINUE on this track of sharing a message I believe so many of us need to hear right now. Let's go back to the Book of Psalms, specifically Psalm 37. This psalm is very close to my heart. The psalmist's words offer a powerful promise as we go from loss to recovery. These verses tell us that even in the midst of seasons that seem as dry and unyielding as famine, God will satisfy you. Look at how the chapter starts: "Fret not thyself because of evildoers.... For they shall soon be cut down like the grass, and wither as the green herb. Trust in the Lord, and do good; so shalt thou dwell in the land....But the meek shall inherit the earth" (Ps. 37:1–3, 11).

Regardless of what's going on—whether it's viruses, violence, or death—the earth is the Lord's. Psalm 24:1 tells us, "The earth is the Lord's, and the fulness thereof; the world, and they that dwell therein." It all belongs to God. The cattle on a thousand hills belong to Him. God is committed to this planet because He is committed to His church. He is committed to preserving it, keeping it, guarding it, and protecting it. We will not be destroyed.

Despite the sicknesses and diseases, economic collapse, and social and political unrest that erupted in 2020, we were not consumed—because of God's people and because of prayer and the spiritual power and authority that we have in the name of Jesus, our Savior. You are still standing. You are still here.

In Psalm 115:16, the Bible says, "The heaven, even the heavens, are the Lord's: but the earth hath he given to the children of men." In other words, God has given us the responsibility to govern, to dominate, to have dominion, and to exercise authority over the earth. And that's what many of us did. At the height of the pandemic and the season of social and political unrest, we took authority over every demon of fear, premature death, destruction, sickness, disease, murder, hatred, violence, indifference, prejudice, and racism, and we bound them. Every demonic spirit operating behind the scenes—every demon causing people to panic, hide, and run—we bound and rebuked in the name of Jesus, trusting God's power to deliver us from it all.

DON'T GET WEARY—GOD KEEPS HIS PROMISES

Depending on what you went through in 2020, it may be an understatement to say the year was a desperate time. What you had to endure may have led to some of the troubles you may be facing now. The same authority that others and perhaps even you took when the world came to a stop is the authority you must take now. Sometimes at the start of the battle we feel strong and have great faith. Yet the longer the battle rages, the weaker and more tired we become. The enemy begins to wear us out. I talk about this "long war" phenomenon in my book *God's Covenant With You for Deliverance and Freedom*. In 2 Samuel 3 we learn that the house of David was in a long war with the house of Saul. The Bible says that as the battle raged, David grew stronger and stronger over time while Saul grew weaker and weaker. I decree that God will strengthen you by His Spirit, and the longer the battle rages, the stronger you will become. You will not get tired. The enemy will not wear you down. You will grow stronger and stronger.

Understand that God will strengthen you even as your season of difficulty wears on. Know that He will also keep you satisfied. In wartime, when battles go on for long periods of time, resources dwindle. Food, weapons, and supplies become scarce. Soldiers go hungry, and some die because of malnourishment and untreated wounds. Morale crashes. But God promises that He will satisfy you in these times. I encourage you to increase your trust in God. Do not grow weary. Wait on the Lord, and He will strengthen your heart. Begin to pray for the Lord's angels to be released on your behalf, to rout the enemy and put him to flight. Pray that God would have mercy and heal all that concerns you.

God is good, and His mercy endures forever. He is compassionate and gracious. God does not forget to show mercy, so ask God to show mercy upon you and your family; your children and loved ones; your finances, church, ministry, and city. This is simply bringing His promise to the forefront.

The Bible says that Jesus gave us authority to tread upon serpents and scorpions and over all the power of the enemy, and nothing shall by any means hurt us (Luke 10:19). So take the authority that God gives to tread upon the enemies of death, fear, discouragement, financial loss, sickness and disease, exhaustion, and whatever the enemy may be throwing at you. Pray for strength. Pray for physical, mental, and emotional healing. Pray for your home to be guarded. Pray for your loved ones. When we pray like this and then remain before God, He will move as a result. Out of seasons of great difficulty come waves of deliverance and salvation. Expect a heavy habitation of God's glory to come. Expect God to meet all of your needs according to His riches in glory (Phil. 4:19). Expect Him to give you more than enough.

Expect God to keep the promise He made in Psalm 37:19—"They shall not be ashamed in the evil time: and in the days of famine they shall be satisfied." You will not be ashamed in the evil time you're facing, in the days where lack and famine seem to rule. Expect that you will be satisfied. I want you to grasp this verse, to confess it. I want you to believe that in the days of famine, in the days of lack, you will be satisfied.

What a powerful scripture Psalm 37:19 is. In many countries people, especially day laborers and farmers, faced hunger when lockdowns shut down economies. We can liken the scarcity to famine. But God has a word for us: you do not have to die in famine; you do not have to suffer like others in famine. Instead, God says that in the days of famine, you will be satisfied.

This almost unbelievable verse of Scripture is in the Bible for a reason. The pandemic and related events were a model for how we can hold on to God during any time the earth experiences famine, lack, or shutdowns. It's a model for anytime the heavens seem to be shut, even over your own life, when nothing is moving. God has promised that in the midst of famine, you will be satisfied. Make this your confession today.

SHAME IS NOT YOUR PORTION

No matter how bad it looks, no matter what the news headlines say, you will not be ashamed in the evil time. You will not be disappointed. God will not forsake you. You will not be the one weeping and crying without any hope. God has given us so many verses that drive home these promises:

> No one who hopes in you will ever be put to shame.
> —Psalm 25:3, NIV

> Do not be afraid; you will not be put to shame. Do not fear disgrace; you will not be humiliated. You will forget the shame of your youth and remember no more the reproach of your widowhood.
> —Isaiah 54:4, NIV

> Behold, I lay in Zion a stumbling stone and rock of offense, and whoever believes on Him will not be put to shame.
> —Romans 9:33, NKJV

> Behold, I am laying in Zion a chosen (honored), precious chief Cornerstone, and he who believes in Him [who adheres to, trusts in, and relies on Him] shall never be disappointed or put to shame.
> —1 Peter 2:6, AMPC

During the pandemic—a type of "evil time"—people were dying. You may have lost someone close to you. Some people were panicking. They didn't know what to do. They were losing their jobs, their income. When times like this come, even when we see that things are not in our control or not our fault, it is hard not to feel embarrassed, ashamed, or humiliated. Sometimes we feel disappointed by God, like He let us down. But I encourage you: trust God and know that these things are not His doing. This psalm is a promise from God that we should use to cast out from our minds the lies of the enemy. It tells us that as God's children, He will not allow shame to come upon us. "You will not be ashamed," He tells us.

His promise can become your confession—any of His promises can. They are all yes and amen to us who are in Christ (2 Cor. 1:20). God is faithful to His promises. Declare:

- I will not be ashamed in the days of famine.
- I will be satisfied.
- I have more than enough.
- God is my provider. He is my more-than-enough, my El Shaddai, my shalom, my protector, and my Deliverer.
- God is the One I can run to and be safe. Under the shadow of His wings, I trust.

- I hide in the secret place, in His pavilion.
- I will not be afraid.
- I will not fall.
- I will not be defeated.
- I have the hand of God, the blessing of God, and the favor of God upon my life.

YOUR WORDS WILL NOT FALL TO THE GROUND

In Job 22:28 we read, "Thou shalt also decree a thing, and it shall be established unto thee." Begin to decree this: "I will not be ashamed. My family will not be ashamed. My loved ones will not be ashamed. My church will not be ashamed. My ministry will not be ashamed. My life will not be ashamed. I trust God. I am a testimony of the goodness of God. I confess the Lord. I depend on God. I will praise and worship. I prophesy His goodness. God will not allow my words to fall to the ground."

About the prophet Samuel, God said not one word of his mouth would fall to the ground (1 Sam. 3:19). God is not going to allow your confession, your word, or your decree to fall to the ground. He will uphold them and this word that I'm giving you today:

- I will not be ashamed in the evil time.
- I will not be ashamed during this season.

- I will not be ashamed during this virus.
- I will not be ashamed during this time of fear and apprehension and people panicking and breaking down.
- I will not be ashamed, and I will not lack.
- I will have more than enough, even in the time of famine.
- God will give me more than enough.
- I will be satisfied in the time of famine.

As you begin to shift from fear to trusting in God's goodness, mercy, grace, and favor in your life, let your faith arise. It is not that we always *feel* like God will make good on His promises; as His children, we know and trust that He will.

DON'T LET FAMINE INTIMIDATE YOU

In the heat of the struggle it's hard to believe what the Scripture says about what God will do for us during these dark times—that He will satisfy us in famine. But I'm going to keep challenging you to grab this word and make it your confession. As a matter of fact, we're going to take it even further. You are going to be so faith-filled and strong that you will laugh at the famine. That's right. Job 5:22 says, "At destruction and famine thou shalt laugh."

Instead of famine being something so dreadful and fearsome that it causes you to fall, faint, bend, or bow before it in defeat, you will laugh. Instead of being afraid of famine, you will laugh at it. Famine will not cause you to die before your time. Despite the famine, you will live and not die.

"Death and life are in the power of the tongue" (Prov. 18:21). So if the Scripture says, "I shall not die, but live, and declare the works of the Lord" (Ps. 118:17), this is what will come out of my mouth. There was a point near the beginning of the pandemic when it looked like the enemy was trying to attack my body. I said, "I will not die. I will live." This is the confession that came out of my mouth, and I encourage you to declare it now too.

DRAW FROM THE STRENGTH OF GOD

There are many ways we can die, just as there are many types of famine. God will sustain and satisfy you through them all. "I have been young, but now am old," the psalmist said, "yet have I not seen the righteous forsaken, nor his seed begging bread" (Ps. 37:25).

Yes, you may have to nurse yourself back to full health after whatever blow you've sustained, but God will give you wisdom to make a full recovery just as He gave my wife and me. I've never been close to dying, and I wasn't at that point when I was ill. It was a sinus condition of some kind. Still, during that time I took care of myself, and my wife nursed me back to health. I stood in faith. I believed God. I came back feeling stronger than ever. God will renew you in whatever type of famine you are facing—physical, mental, spiritual, financial, or relational. He will cause you to come back stronger than ever.

The Scripture says, "Bless the Lord....Who satisfies your mouth with good things, so that your youth is renewed like the eagle's" (Ps. 103:1,5, NKJV). Then Isaiah 40:31 tells us, "But those who wait on the Lord shall renew their strength; they shall mount up with wings like eagles, they shall run and not be weary, they shall walk and not faint" (NKJV).

Believe the Lord is the strength of your life, that He is going to renew your strength. Believe for more strength than you've ever had before in spite of anything that has come against you. Believe that the Lord will give you the strength you had as a youth.

Building faith and expectancy for God's promises to manifest in your life begins with your mouth. It begins with words. It begins with the weak saying, "I am strong." (See Joel 3:10.) If you feel weak, say, "I'm strong." Declare, "The Lord is the strength of my life. The Lord is my light and my salvation. The Lord gives me strength. My strength is from God. The Lord gives me power. The spirit of might, power, and strength is my portion."

I want you to speak and believe that during the days of famine, you will be satisfied. You will not lack during this season, and you will not be ashamed. God will not allow you to be put to shame. He will provide for you and take care of you.

Just as the height of the pandemic will come and go in the United States, this season you are in will pass too. What you are going through right now will come to an end. New glory, power, and strength will come upon you. God has to make room for it in your life, as we discussed in chapter 2. Things cannot remain the same, but God will sustain you and give you strength.

The Scripture tells us, "If thou faint in the day of adversity, thy strength is small" (Prov. 24:10). You cannot faint during the time of adversity. Instead, you need to draw from the strength of God. By the power of the Holy Ghost and the anointing of God, I speak life to you. I speak healing. I speak restoration. I speak strength. I speak favor. I speak grace. I speak divine protection over your life in this season.

Remember: believe God's prophets and you will prosper. God gave me these words for you in the midst of a pandemic, yet He showed me that as we go higher in Him, there will be seasons where we may experience individual or personal pandemics, shutdowns, and famines. The anointing and authority we used collectively to pray against spirits of disease and premature death is the same authority we have individually when we're dealing with difficult seasons.

As a prophet of God, I declare to you, believe God

for a divine turnaround. His strength will sustain you. Though things may feel touch-and-go at various times, God promises you will lack no good thing. Remain faithful. Keep giving and sowing. Stay in the Word and pray with all kinds of prayer. Fear God and be wise. Your life will get back on track.

CHAPTER 5

FROM LEAST TO GREATEST

O my Lord, how can I save Israel? Indeed my clan is the weakest in Manasseh, and I am the least in my father's house.
—Judges 6:15, NKJV

There are almost eight billion people on the planet at the time of this writing, and all eight billion of us dream. Dreams are very important. Scientists have discovered that dreams are one of the ways God heals us. Through the dream cycle He restores us from trauma and things we go through in life and throughout our day.

Researchers at UC Berkeley have found that when dreams occur during the REM (rapid eye movement) stage of sleep, our stress responses shut down, and the release of neurochemicals responsible for stressful feelings are halted. Not only this, but REM also helps reduce the negative effects of difficult memories.

> "The dream stage of sleep, based on its unique neurochemical composition, provides us with a form of overnight therapy, a soothing balm that removes the sharp edges from the prior day's emotional experiences," said Matter Walker, PhD, the senior author of the study that was published in November in *Current Biology*.[1]

Scientists have also determined that we dream every night, even though most of us don't remember what we dream. Think about it: every one of us dreams, yet each of our dreams is unique. No two people have exactly the same dream, because the dream is something based on our unique life situation and what we go through. I'm sure you've had dreams so crazy you had no idea what they meant. Sometimes when a dream is especially confusing or poignant, we look for ways to interpret it.

The Scripture says that interpretations belong to God (Gen. 40:8). He is the One who gives skill and understanding of how to interpret dreams. When we understand our dreams, we can receive counsel from God. Psalm 16:7 says, "I will bless the LORD who counsels me—even at night when my thoughts trouble me" (CSB). God will give us counsel, wisdom, and instruction.

Through our dreams He brings healing, answers, and solutions to the things we're dealing with in life.

For most of us who sleep eight hours a night, we're sleeping one-third of our lives. This means that God has a lot of opportunity to speak to us and bring restoration into our lives spiritually, emotionally, and physically.

In this chapter I will discuss a specific dream in Scripture recorded in the Book of Judges. It's a dream that a man had about a Hebrew leader named Gideon during a battle between Israel and Midian. I didn't have a full picture of this dream until I listened to another minister teach on it. Studying this dream really opened my eyes.

Gideon was a man who saw himself as small and insignificant. He came from the weakest clan in Manasseh, and among them he was the least. God called him to lead a company of men to overtake one of Israel's enemies. Gideon was overwhelmed by the task and did not see how he could do it. Even after God said He'd be with him, Gideon was afraid. It wasn't until he heard a man talking about a dream he'd had of Gideon's victory that he was able to muster the strength and courage to go out and take the enemy.

Often we find ourselves in difficult circumstances, much like the one that may have brought you to this book. We may be weighing the pros and cons of a difficult decision or trying to figure out how to rebound after financial loss or the end of a significant relationship. As a result of a hardship or difficulty we've endured, we may be struggling with anxiety, fear, insecurity, or depression. We may need direction, peace, clarity, and even deliverance. God can speak solutions, comfort, confirmation, direction, encouragement, and answers to our prayers through dreams. Just as God provided what Gideon needed to carry out his call, God can give you the right dream at the right time to put you back on track toward restoration and victory.

Job 33 contains several of my favorite Scripture verses about God's purpose for dreams:

> For God speaks again and again, though people do not recognize it. He speaks in dreams, in visions of the night, when deep sleep falls on people as they lie in their beds. He whispers in their ears.
> —Job 33:14–16, NLT

Here we see biblical proof that God speaks often in dreams and visions. The problem is that we may not perceive what God is saying because most dreams are symbolic, not literal or concrete. That's why they sometimes appear to be so crazy. God can, of course, give you a dream and literally tell you something, but understanding the symbols of your dreams will help you interpret what God is trying to tell you.

DREAMS UNLOCK WISDOM AND UNDERSTANDING

Sometimes because dreams can be so symbolic, we may be quick to dismiss and forget them. I recommend that you try to remember your dreams. Keep a journal by your bed and write down each dream, especially if you dream a lot. Write down the details: What are the figures in the dream? Who are the people? What did you see and feel? Were you afraid or anxious? Were you joyful, happy, or excited?

Knowing these details can help you to begin deciphering what God may be telling you as you go through certain seasons of life, especially difficult ones where the path to victory is not coming clearly through the normal channels of revelation. God will give you wisdom to do it. I believe that dream interpretation comes through wisdom. Daniel and Joseph are individuals in the Bible who were able to interpret the dreams of kings, and they were known for their wisdom. Wisdom is the principal thing. Wisdom is the ability.

Proverbs 1 says that part of the work of those who have wisdom and understanding is "to understand a proverb, and the interpretation; the words of the wise, and their dark sayings" (v. 6).

The word *dark* refers to something that's hidden—"hidden sayings," as some Bible versions translate it. To interpret these hidden meanings, you need the wisdom that comes from God.

I believe the spirit of wisdom is going to be released. Toward the end of this chapter we're going to pray for the spirit of wisdom so we can understand parables, symbolic speech, heaven's language, and the language of pictures. I see it as a movie lens.

PARABLES, PICTURES, AND SYMBOLS

Did you ever watch the movie *The Matrix*? I had a hard time figuring out what this movie was about because it was so symbolic. The movie's main themes were communicated like a parable. The same thing applies to dreams.

God can give you a dream. In your dream you could be in a car, a boat, or a ship. You could be moving forward. Or maybe you're not moving forward: you have a flat tire, or the wheels are falling off the car. Or maybe it's not you in the dream; it's your pastor or a father or mother figure. Maybe it's a friend. Maybe the person in your dream is not someone you know. You can have dreams with celebrities in them or people you've seen on television. And sometimes it's what that person represents and not really about who they are in real life.

While the dream realm is a realm of parables and symbols, God can also give you a literal dream as He did with Joseph, the father of Jesus. In a dream, God told Joseph to take his son and go to Egypt to save the life of the child Jesus. That was the literal dream.

Like Joseph's dream, many dreams are influenced by something in your life that you are presently dealing with. In real life, there was life-threatening danger on the horizon. Herod wanted to kill all boys under two years old. What would they do to keep Jesus safe? The answer came in a dream.

An issue you are dealing with in your heart can also prompt a dream. It can be a problem or a situation, something that is causing you stress or is difficult for you to overcome. You may dream about it. Recognize the dream as God's way of giving you counsel or guidance for how to overcome or handle the issue or situation.

I believe God uses dreams because often during the day we're so busy working and conducting business, we're not really positioned to clearly hear everything He wants to tell us. God waits until we go to sleep and we're resting, and then He downloads His vision, counsel, and instruction into our hearts through a dream. All we have to do is be able to interpret the dream's symbols.

In other dreams God reveals the future. These kinds of dreams can be prophetic and about the next season of your life.

A DEMONSTRATION OF LOVE

God loves us so much. He's concerned about our lives. He's concerned about what we're dealing with, and He will speak to us and give us answers and counsel through dreams that bring resolution, victory, and deliverance out of the issues that trouble us. As prophetic people, we want to live in this realm because of the great breakthroughs, miracles, counsel, wisdom, and direction it brings into our lives. We're not left to struggle in life, trying to figure things out on our own.

Sometimes people tell me they're praying about and asking God for answers and solutions, but they feel as if God doesn't care about them because He doesn't seem to answer their prayers. Often I counsel them to pay attention to their dreams. God may actually be speaking loudly.

Sometimes it's easy to ignore or brush off dreams, especially when they're crazy: "That was a crazy dream. I must have had too much pizza." But many times it's God trying to bring you answers to your prayers and solutions for your problems. Again, God is concerned about your life. He loves you. He doesn't want you to be overcome with the problems of life and the difficulties in relationships, business, or ministry. Your heart issues, fears, struggles, things that you're coming up against, things you're failing at, things that are frustrating you, and things you can't figure out—all these matter to God. He hears your prayers: "How do I overcome this? How do I break through that?" To come to your rescue, God can give you a dream—and sometimes a series of dreams over a period of time—that will offer you the answers, counsel, and wisdom you need.

I encourage you to believe God for these dreams, especially if you are walking through a dark season. I want you to ask Him for His wisdom and insight into this realm so that you won't be afraid of it. Often we draw back from and shut down the things of God we don't understand. In doing this, we sometimes miss out on His bountiful benefits.

Of course there are dreams that don't come from God—nightmares, night terrors, and other terrifying dreams. These can sometimes be demonic. That's why we're going to pray at the end of this chapter that the Holy Spirit will increase your wisdom and discernment. You want to be able to guard against the enemy's counterfeits. Satan wants to keep you in fear and disbelief so that you do not gain the benefits of communing with God in this area.

A dream from God can save your life. A dream can encourage and give you wisdom and strategy. A dream can even give you an idea or invention, or show you details you need to know about something you're working on or pursuing.

INTERPRETING YOUR DREAMS

One of the first steps to interpreting your dream is to try to place it within the context of what you're dealing with. Ask yourself, "What is going on in my life? How does this dream apply to what I'm dealing with? What's happening in my relationships, business, finances, or ministry? What's happening in my emotions or heart? What am I afraid of? What am I struggling with?" Is it a habit or sin, guilt, shame, condemnation, sadness, depression, or discouragement?

Next, look at the individuals in your dream. What could they represent?

People have told me I was in their dreams. While that's flattering, I know I have not appeared in their dreams as only a representation of myself. A lot of people watch me on Facebook or have heard me speak when I travel around the nation and the world, so I may appear in their dreams simply because of the role I fill in the body of Christ. I could represent the apostolic ministry or maybe some kind of authority figure. I could represent deliverance because that's what I'm known for. I could represent the prophetic or someone who's a father in the faith or a pioneer.

You can dream about your own pastor, who may represent authority or power; sometimes your pastor can even represent God. Your pastor, of course, is not God, but he or she may be representing God's authority and power in your dream. Maybe you dream about your father, who may represent God, because God is your Father. Maybe you dream about a friend; your friend could represent Jesus, because Jesus is a friend who sticks closer than a brother. Sometimes you have a dream with different people in it, and while you may be led to believe the dream is about them, it may not be at all. It may be more about what they represent.

Just remember that God uses people and pictures to give us messages.

Then notice any symbols. They represent different things to different people. A serpent, for example, is often recognized as the devil, which Scripture corroborates: "I give unto you power to tread on serpents and scorpions" (Luke 10:19). A serpent can also represent wisdom. Scripture says, "Be wise as serpents and harmless as doves" (Matt. 10:16, NKJV). So be very careful that you just don't jump and say that something represents a demon. It could represent something holy or of value to the person who dreamed about it.

What about a lion? Have you ever had a dream with a lion in it? On one hand, it could represent Jesus—He is the Lion of Judah. On the other hand, the devil is characterized as a roaring lion in Scripture.

A symbol's meaning can differ from person to person because our experiences are different. As I already mentioned, dreams usually follow what you are dealing with presently in your life. So you have to use your circumstances as clues to understand what a symbol could mean to you. You have a history. Certain things represent certain things, which may also have certain emotions attached to them. For instance, if you see a dog in your dream—some people love dogs—it might represent companionship. Someone else may have been bitten by a dog, so he is afraid of dogs and doesn't particularly care for them. So for him, dogs can represent something threatening or fear-inducing.

Each of us has different symbols in our dreams that connect with certain times in our lives or even emotions. We can use this knowledge to help us understand the symbolism in our dreams, at least in a general way.

Finally, as you begin to look at your dreams in this light, don't limit God. He can use a lot of different symbols from your everyday life to speak to you—shows or movies you've watched, conversations you've had, books you've read, your likes and dislikes, things that bring you joy or cause you to fear, vacations you've taken or wish to take, and more. His greatest desire for speaking to you in your dreams is to bring some type of comfort, healing, resolution, and counsel to your life.

GOING FROM LEAST TO GREATEST

I don't think we really know the power of dreams because very few churches teach in this area. When is the last time you heard teaching on dreams in your local church? Most pastors don't deal with it. In fact if you report having a lot of dreams, some churches will make you feel as if you're weird and spooky. Let me assure you that you're not. You are simply experiencing another of God's methods of communication. And do be mindful: Dreams never replace the Spirit of God. Prophecy never replaces the Spirit of God or the leading of the Holy Ghost. They are great tools that God can use. I'm not suggesting that dreams take precedent over the Word of God or the Spirit of God in your life. Stay connected to both His Word and His Spirit, and go to Him as you try to figure out and navigate this realm. Remember that interpretation belongs to God.

We've already talked about Gideon as a leader, but let's look at the dream that started it all and crystallized God's call on Gideon's life. He was a young man when God found him threshing grain and hiding it in a winepress so the Midianites wouldn't find it. God saw Gideon and called him out for his greatness even though we learn right away that Gideon did not feel great about himself at all. God addressed him as "mighty man of valor" (Judg. 6:12). But Gideon was fearful. Upon hearing God call him to be the one who would lead Israel to victory against the Midianites, Gideon answered, "O my Lord, how can I save Israel? Indeed my clan is the weakest in Manasseh, and I am the least in my father's house" (Judg. 6:15, NKJV).

Gideon was not a fighter or a warrior. He was very afraid, so he set out fleeces before the Lord to confirm what God was telling him to do. God answered his request, proving to Gideon that he was indeed the man for the mission. When Gideon assembled a large army, God told him he had too many people. After a while, God told him to take his militia down to three hundred people. Now Gideon was already afraid to go into battle, and suddenly he had just three hundred men to go against thousands of Midianites. As you can imagine, Gideon was afraid. He was intimidated, and God knew this. Notice that God did not eliminate Gideon or tell him he was no longer qualified because he was afraid. Instead He told Gideon:

> Arise, go down against the camp, for I have delivered it into your hand. But if you are afraid to go down, go down to the camp with Purah your servant, and you shall hear what they say; and afterward your hands shall be strengthened to go down against the camp.
> —Judges 7:9–11, NKJV

Gideon obeyed.

> And when Gideon had come, there was a man telling a dream to his companion. He said, "I have had a dream: To my surprise, a loaf of barley bread tumbled into the camp of Midian; it came to a tent and struck it so that it fell and overturned, and the tent collapsed."
> Then his companion answered and said, "This is nothing else but the sword of Gideon, the son of Joash, a man of Israel! Into his hand God has delivered Midian and the whole camp."
> —Judges 7:13–14, NKJV

God used this dream to help Gideon overcome his fear. Notice that it was not Gideon's dream, per se. He simply heard an individual talking to another about the dream. The person who heard the dream gave the interpretation that this barley cake that was tumbling into the camp and flattening tents was none other than Gideon. The dream was a picture of Gideon coming into the enemy's camp and destroying and defeating it. God used a barley cake to symbolize Gideon. We're going to look back at this in a moment, but first let's go on to the next verse:

> And so it was, when Gideon heard the telling of the dream and its interpretation, that he worshiped. He returned to the camp of Israel, and said, "Arise, for the LORD has delivered the camp of Midian into your hand."
> —JUDGES 7:15, NKJV

God used this dream to give Gideon the confirmation that victory was his and there was nothing to fear. Sometimes this is all we need—to see the victory already won. If you read further into the next few verses, you'll see that Gideon had a strategy. He knew what to do with the men God had given him. Maybe you have a good idea what your next step should be, but you need that push from God confirming the victory is yours. Maybe He will do this for you through a dream as well.

Gideon's victory became one of Israel's greatest victories in the Book of Judges. He lived up to the "mighty man of valor" name God gave him.

Before we leave this story, I want you to notice how God uses symbolism. The man who dreamed about

Gideon's victory saw a barley cake coming into the camp. Notice he didn't see a sword or a horse. He didn't see a chariot. He saw a barley cake tumble into the camp and flatten a tent. Now why didn't God just show him Gideon coming in with the sword? Why didn't God just show three hundred men charging in and destroying the Midianites? Why would God use a barley cake as a symbol of Gideon? Because again, dreams are symbolic.

A piece of bread is not usually used to destroy an enemy. That's the last thing you use to fight with. Bread is soft. It breaks down. You don't go to battle with a loaf of bread. You don't go to fight with a cake. You go with a sword or some kind of weapon. This symbol of a barley cake goes back to God calling Gideon to lead those men. Gideon was making grain they used to bake cakes with. A cake could possibly represent weakness, something you wouldn't use in a battle to defeat the enemy. Knowing the context, we can see how the cake may be a symbol for Gideon, who felt as though he was the weakest and the least of the least.

Of all the people God would choose, He chose the least of the least to destroy the enemy. God showed Gideon that he may have been the least of the least, he may have been weak, but just like David went against the Philistines with only a slingshot, God uses the weak things of the world to confound the mighty (1 Cor. 1:27).

So it turns out that in this case, the barley cake was an apt symbol. Its appearance in the dream helped Gideon overcome his fear and intimidation.

DREAMING OF VICTORY

Sometimes when you're weak, you can look down on yourself and feel you can't do what God has called you to do. You can't see sure victory. Just as He gave Gideon the interpretation of another's dream, God can give you a dream to symbolically show you He's going to use you to get it done. He says, "In spite of your weakness, in spite of your insignificance, and in spite of the fact that you are the least of the least, I will help you overcome this feeling of inadequacy—because I'm God, and I can use you. I delight in taking the least of the least to get the job done."

Even beyond fear, God will give you a dream based on what you're dealing with in your life. If you're apprehensive, discouraged, or frustrated, God can give you a dream to help you overcome those emotions. You can get deliverance from a dream. God can deliver you in a dream, and you can wake up set free or released from certain things.

Remember the Creator of the dream cycle. In His wisdom, compassion, and creativity God gave us dreams. Don't be afraid to ask God, "What does this symbol mean? What does it represent to me? What is it about this symbol that You want to show me?" God wants to give you counsel, strength, encouragement, deliverance, and the ability to overcome and break through. He doesn't want you to suffer through life feeling alone like one who has no guidance and direction.

Let God speak to you concerning that thing you're dealing with at the present time. He has victory in store for you even through your dreams.

PRAYER FOR ACTIVATING YOUR DREAM LIFE

Dear heavenly Father,

You are so awesome. Thank You for Your heart for us and that You always want to connect with us. Thank You so much for dreams and communicating to us through them.

If we Your people have not honored dreams in the past, we repent for that. I change my thinking to line up with Your thoughts and perspective, God. I know You spoke in the Bible through dreams over and over again and that You want to do the same thing in our lives today (Job 33:14–18).

By Your grace, I purpose in my heart to honor dreams and receive Your revelation through them. I know interpretations belong to You, and I thank You for Your Spirit's power that helps us remember our dreams and translate Your messages through them (Gen. 40:8; John 14:26).

God, I see in Scripture how You not only spoke through dreams but even spoke through nightmares (Gen. 15:12–14). I see how You warn and protect us through these dreams, so I choose to honor them too (Matt. 2:22). Thank You, Father, that You transform bad dreams into blessings. I purpose to hear from You through all of my dreams and act according to Your counsel.

Your Word says You give to Your beloved in our sleep (Ps. 127:2). Thank You that You declared You would reveal Yourself to us in visions and promised You would speak to us in dreams (Num. 12:6). Thank You that Your Word says You visit us in the night and give our hearts counsel and instruction while we sleep (Ps. 17:3; 16:7).

I pray that the eyes of my heart would be enlightened, that I would see You and hear You in my visions of the night (Eph. 1:18). Father God, thank You that the dream is certain and its interpretation sure, and that You will do whatever is necessary to get Your message to us because You love us so much (Dan. 2:45).

Father, thank You for Your relentless pursuit of our hearts. Thank You that when we are asleep, our hearts are awake to commune with You, our Beloved (Song of Sol. 5:2). Thank You for Your contingency plan of dreams. You are amazing, God. You thought of everything!

We love You so much, we honor You, and we bless You. In Jesus' name I pray, amen.[2]

CHAPTER 6

LET YOUR HEART BE ENLARGED

And God gave Solomon wisdom and understanding exceeding much, and largeness of heart, even as the sand that is on the sea shore.

—1 Kings 4:29

When life is beating us down or we are living in the consequences of repeated mistakes, or just at a difficult crossroads, we may pray for wisdom: "Lord, give me exceeding wisdom"; "Lord, give me great wisdom"; "Lord, pour Your wisdom into me." We know wisdom is vital. We know that wisdom is connected to the enormous wealth and renown that Solomon experienced. We want the ability to live prosperously and in the abundance Jesus came to give us. We want to live the results of good decision making and success. Wisdom brings all of this and more. But are our hearts large enough to receive what God can pour out? Do we have the spiritual capacity to contain it?

When God blessed Solomon, He not only gave him exceeding wisdom, but He also gave him a big heart. He gave him a heart so large it was compared to the sand on the seashore. This part of the verse caught my attention. As I began to read and study it, I asked God, "What does 'largeness of heart' mean?" He answered, saying, "Capacity. What is your capacity?"

The word *capacity* means "the maximum amount or number that can be contained or accommodated."[1] A drinking glass, for instance, only has a certain capacity to hold water. You can only put as much in it as it can hold. It is limited. Of course you can get another glass with a larger capacity and it will hold more, but not more than it is made to hold.

So how much wisdom can you carry in your heart? What is your spiritual capacity? Do you have a large heart?

LIKE THE SAND ON THE SEASHORE

Solomon was able to contain much or "exceeding" wisdom because God not only gave him wisdom, but He also gave him the capacity to hold this kind of wisdom. The verse says his heart was enlarged even as the sand of the sea. Now that's an unusual way of saying it. Can you imagine the size of this man's heart—not physically, but spiritually?

God spoke to Abraham in similar terms. He said, "I am going to multiply you as the sands of the sea." (See Genesis 22:17.) In other words, "You're not going to be able to measure the amount by which I'm going to multiply you." By this we can understand that Solomon's heart was almost unmeasurable. I can't completely understand this. The kind of heart this man must have had and the level and amount of wisdom he was able to contain is truly mind blowing.

Solomon wrote more than one thousand songs and three thousand-plus proverbs, which shows he had almost an unlimited amount of wisdom. The amount of wisdom a person carries depends on the size or largeness of his or her heart.

In this I hear God saying, "My wisdom is unlimited." We can't measure the wisdom God has. We can't measure the amount of wisdom a person can carry. God can pour into you—depending on your capacity and the size of your heart—an immeasurable amount of wisdom. This verse really challenges me that not only do I need a big heart, a large heart, but I also need to ask God to enlarge my capacity even more.

There is something more to this. As I studied this idea of "enlarging our hearts to hold an immeasurable amount of God's wisdom," I found that the word *heart* is mentioned more in the Books of Psalms and Proverbs than any other books in the Bible. In the

King James Version the word *heart* appears 130 times in the Book of Psalms and 82 times in the Book of Proverbs. In the Book of Psalms the word is primarily connected to worship, which shows us that worship is a heart issue. You worship God from your heart.

YOUR HEART IS NOT EVIL; IT'S NEW

I want to do some corrective teaching that will adjust some of what you've heard in the church, which I believe is incorrect teaching concerning the heart. Most of us have heard the Scripture verse that says, "The heart is...desperately wicked: who can know it?" (Jer. 17:9). Most Christians believe that their hearts are desperately wicked. But the problem with that is this: Ezekiel prophesied that God would give us new hearts and that He would put a new spirit within us (Ezek. 36:26). So for us to say that our hearts are desperately wicked is not true.

If you're a believer, God has given you a new heart. Continuing to think your heart is desperately wicked is, I believe, incorrect theology. My heart is not desperately wicked. It may have been desperately wicked at one time, but I am born-again now. God has actually given me a new heart. He gives you a new heart as well when you accept Him. So stop walking around saying, "You know, our hearts are desperately wicked. You don't know what's in your heart. It's evil." No. You have a new heart, according to the Word of God.

Ezekiel prophesied that under the new covenant, God would put a new heart in you. It's called being born-again. You are born of the Spirit. John 3:6 says, "That which is born of the flesh is flesh; and that which is born of the Spirit is spirit." I call the spirit the hidden man of the heart. I have a new heart, you have a new heart, and God has put His Spirit inside us.

Though your heart is not wicked, you can still walk and do things in the flesh. But if you live in the Spirit and follow your heart, which is new, you will walk in the Spirit. In 2 Corinthians 5:17 Paul writes, "If anyone is in Christ, he is a new creation" (NKJV). Your heart is the new creation. God takes the heart of stone out and puts in a heart of flesh. So stop believing the teaching that says your heart is desperately wicked. Even saying that your righteousness is as filthy rags is not exactly right when you consider that you no longer have your righteousness; you have the righteousness of Christ. *He* is now your righteousness. You cannot be justified by your righteous deeds. As a believer, you now have the righteousness of Christ.

We need to make these adjustments in our theology so we are not new covenant believers still operating under the old covenant—the law—when people did not have new hearts. They still had stony, sinful, and rebellious hearts. Thank God for the new creation, for the new birth. Thank Him that He comes in and puts a new heart inside of us and now wants to enlarge it so it can hold His wisdom and love for Him, ourselves, and other people. I believe all of this is a result of the new birth.

MAKE ROOM

Largeness has to do with making enough room. It means "having more than usual capacity or scope."² You should have room for people. You should have room in your heart for many different areas of wisdom. Your heart should be able to contain revelation, wisdom, counsel, understanding, and knowledge. You should know about the prophetic, the apostolic, deliverance, glory, worship, prosperity, giving, intercession, faith—all these different areas that God has given to us. He gave us the ability to embrace those truths in our hearts because when you are born-again and God gives you a new heart, He also gives you a large heart. So we have the capacity to walk in a greater degree of wisdom.

One of the first things wisdom tells us in Proverbs 4:4, 21 is "Let thine heart retain my words....Let them not depart from thine eyes; keep them in the midst of thine heart." Then Proverbs 7:1–3 says, "Keep my words....Bind them upon thy fingers, write them upon the table of thine heart." So you can write upon your heart through your words. David said his tongue was the "pen of a ready writer" (Ps. 45:1).

Romans 10:8 says, "The word is nigh thee, even in thy mouth, and in thy heart: that is, the word of faith, which we preach." This verse tells us that the more you confess the Word of God, the more you're writing it upon your heart, and the more wisdom fills your heart and stretches its capacity. So begin quoting these wisdom scriptures. Say them aloud.

- Christ is my wisdom.
- I have the wisdom of Christ inside me.
- I have the spirit of wisdom because I have the Holy Spirit dwelling inside me.
- I walk in wisdom because I have the fear of the Lord, and the fear of the Lord is the beginning of wisdom.
- I exalt wisdom, and wisdom exalts me.
- I make wisdom my kinswoman and my partner.
- Wisdom will fill my treasuries.
- Wisdom will bring me riches and honor.
- Wisdom will promote me.
- Wisdom will lengthen my days.

Write these scriptures on your heart by confessing them. Wisdom is connected to the heart. The heart of the wicked goes after foolishness, but the heart of the righteous seeks wisdom. Wisdom is a heart issue. The measure of wisdom you walk in depends on your heart, on whether or not you are born-again. When you have a new heart—a heart of flesh—you have a heart that has the capacity to receive more wisdom.

Think about this: I know people who have read thousands of books. I've read thousands of books. To do this, I had to have a large heart, a large mind. (Sometimes the word *heart* is also connected to the mind.) The Hebrew word *leb* means both "heart" and "mind."[3] God had to give me a large mind to read about so many different subjects to teach and preach over these last almost forty years. I've studied so many different subjects in Scripture—I'm still studying. I'm still enlarging. I'm still getting more in my heart. I've read books on the prophetic, deliverance, healing, prosperity, faith, intercession, dreams, vision, glory, Zion—so many different subjects—books on mercy, compassion, authority, warfare, casting out demons, the Holy Spirit. To deposit that much knowledge, I need a large mind or heart.

Now, if you read one book and said, "Oh, my God, I can't handle any more," then evidently your heart is not large. Your mind is not large. Let me say it this way: Don't be narrow-minded. Don't be small-minded. Have a big heart.

Having a big heart also means that you have a capacity to operate in love, mercy, and compassion—you love people, and you open your heart to them. God increased Solomon's capacity in all these areas, and He can do the same for you. God can give you largeness of heart if you ask Him. You can ask Him to give you greater capacity for more revelation, wisdom, knowledge, and understanding, because what God can teach you, show you, and impart to you is unlimited.

On this earth there are large bodies of water and small ones. I live in Chicago on what are called the Great Lakes—Lake Superior, Lake Michigan, Lake Huron, Lake Ontario, and Lake Erie—some of the largest lakes in the world. They're known for their capacity and for being some of the largest reservoirs of fresh water in America. Then there are the oceans, which are even larger, with their salt water—the Pacific Ocean, the largest ocean, with trillions of gallons of water, as well as the Atlantic, Indian, and Arctic Oceans. These large bodies of water are reservoirs.

Your heart is a reservoir. It is a container. Your heart can contain wisdom, revelation, and knowledge. It can contain love, compassion, mercy, power, insight, and understanding. It can contain songs and books. You can write books and volumes from your heart, depending on its capacity.

It's interesting that God gave Solomon largeness of heart. It's as if He was saying, "Listen, Solomon. If you're going to handle the amount of wisdom, knowledge, and understanding I'm about to deposit in you, I must enlarge your heart. Your heart is not big enough to contain it all."

You've met people like this; they are containers of knowledge and wisdom. Then you meet some people who are very narrow-minded. Narrow-minded people tend to harbor prejudice. They have small hearts. They don't know very much. They're limited in their understanding. But God wants to give you a large heart. He wants to expand your mind and understanding. He wants to give you more wisdom. But your capacity to receive this "exceeding much" wisdom depends on the size of your heart.

God is unlimited. He has enough wisdom to fill everyone. But He is saying, "The limitation is not with Me; it's the size of your heart." He says, "If any of you lack wisdom, let him ask of God, that giveth to all men liberally" (Jas. 1:5). You limit the amount of wisdom God can give you based on the condition of your heart.

THE ANOINTING ENLARGES YOUR HEART

Psalm 119:32 says, "I will run the way of thy commandments, when thou shalt enlarge my heart." An enlarged heart also gives you the ability to obey and run after God's commandments. You have room in your heart for the commandments of God and for the Word of God. You have room in your heart for how much Word you can walk in and receive. How much revelation you can receive depends on the size of your heart. Remember, we have new hearts, so we have the capacity under the new covenant to walk in this. Every new Spirit-filled believer has the capacity to walk in it. If you're a new covenant believer, you have a new heart.

You have the Spirit of God in you, and the Spirit of God can enlarge your heart.

Sometimes as you're baptized in the Holy Ghost, God enlarges your heart. For example, when Saul met the company of prophets, the Bible says "God gave him another heart" (1 Sam. 10:9), and a few verses earlier we read that he was "turned into another man" (v. 6). So when you come in contact with the prophetic, God can enlarge your heart. Certain anointings enlarge your heart and give you a greater spiritual capacity. I believe that apostolic and prophetic anointings are designed to help build greater capacity in you. Christ is the Anointed One, and through Him the anointing upon men and women of God enlarges our hearts to obey and walk in God's commandments.

Sometimes we come into a church or a ministry and our hearts are a certain dimension, but God begins to enlarge our hearts just through our exposure to the church's different kinds of anointings.

WORD OF THE LORD CONCERNING ENLARGING YOUR HEART

I love what God says to His people in Isaiah 54:2–3: "Enlarge the place of thy tent, and let them stretch forth the curtains of thine habitations: spare not, lengthen thy cords, and strengthen thy stakes; for thou shalt break forth on the right hand and on the left."

God is ready to release some new wisdom. He's

ready to enlarge your revelation of riches, wealth, and giving. He is ready to give you a greater ability to give and receive. He's ready to pour more revelation, more wisdom, more knowledge, and more understanding into you than you've ever known before. You're about to grow and increase in your level of wisdom in the next six months, even the next six years.

You are about to get a download of wisdom. Have you ever gone shopping for a new computer? One of the first questions they ask is, "How much storage do you need?" Some computers have a greater capacity, a greater amount of available storage than others. You can get by with a small computer with small capacity if you don't have a lot to put on it. But the more movies and data you need to put on a device, the more room you need. You don't need gigabytes; you need terabytes.

It's the same way with us. We're like that hard drive. How much room, how much capacity do you need? The more wisdom, knowledge, and understanding God is downloading to you, the more He'll need to expand your hard drive. He needs to expand your heart. You have too much vision, too many dreams, too many words, too much revelation—too much—that you need to store. So I want you to believe that God will enlarge your heart even as the sand on the seashore.

I hear the Lord saying:

> Allow Me to enlarge your heart, your spiritual capacity. I'm putting more wisdom, more

knowledge, more understanding, and more revelation inside of you so that you may be able to live with a greater capacity. Get ready. With your enlarged heart, you're going to break out on the right hand and on the left. You're lengthening your cord and strengthening your stakes. You're making more room for Me to pour into you and bless you.

There are many things you can't handle until I enlarge you on the inside. Before you walk in greater finances, larger ministries or platforms, I have to do a work inside of you. I'm giving you a new heart, and through the Holy Spirit, I'm giving you a big heart, a heart of flesh. It'll be the work of My Spirit. You'll be changed into another person. I desire to pour so much into you. I desire to give you so much more. I desire to fill you up and cause you to overflow. I desire to give you the ability and the capacity to receive fully what I'm releasing in your life in this hour. So get ready for the outpouring. Get ready for Me to fill you up with wisdom, knowledge, and understanding to live the life I've destined you to live.

PRAYER FOR GREATER HEART CAPACITY

Father, I pray for enlargement today. I pray, Lord, that You would give me the "exceeding much wisdom" that You gave to Solomon because he asked You. Give me largeness of heart.

Lord, You are no respecter of persons. Give me what You gave Solomon. Jesus is inside of me. He is my wisdom. Let Christ, the Anointed One, give me a large heart and increase my wisdom.

Father, I give You praise. I give You glory. I thank You, Lord, that You're pouring out a large amount of wisdom. You're increasing my capacity. You're expanding me.

Make my heart large enough to receive wisdom in finances, wisdom in business, wisdom in relationships, wisdom in my family, wisdom in ministry—wisdom in everything I do.

Increase my capacity to receive more, and let there be an outpouring, a downpour, and a release of the spirit of wisdom. I thank You, Lord, for largeness of heart. I am believing for it. I decree that my heart is large. I have a greater capacity to receive all that God has for me. Thank You, Jesus! Amen.

CHAPTER 7

RESTORING HONOR

*A good name is more desirable
than great riches.*

—PROVERBS 22:1, NIV

IN THE LAST chapter we discussed the connection between wisdom and largeness of heart—that for you to be ready to receive what God has for you as you get in position for recovery, you must have the capacity to contain it. God gives us the capacity for "exceeding much" wisdom. We need as much wisdom as we can hold so that we can live in the blessings that wisdom brings into our lives. In His Word, God has given us wisdom on many different areas of our lives because our lives are multifaceted and multidimensional. You have family. You may have a business. You attend or lead a church or ministry. You have relationships. Wisdom covers an abundance of areas because it is what will help you avoid making mistakes that will bring shame and destruction. In this chapter we'll focus on how wisdom helps us avoid or recover from shame.

The Scriptures tell us that wisdom will bring us honor and promotion. It is very important that you live an honorable life, that your name has honor. The Bible says, "A good name is better than riches" (Prov. 22:1, author's paraphrase). It's also important that you have a good reputation.

Honor is respect. Honor is when people bless you. When people hear your name or interact with you, there's nothing dishonorable about your life.

There are some people who don't care about honor. They don't care what anybody thinks about them. They feel they can do what they want to do. But you should care about having a good name. You should care that people think honorably toward you and respect you. God cares about how you are honored. It's a reflection on Him—good or bad.

The opposite of honor is dishonor, shame, or humiliation. Now, I'm going to approach this from a deliverance point of view, as well as from the view of wisdom. I want to share with you how shame is mentioned throughout Proverbs. God does not want your life to end in shame. He doesn't want you to experience humiliating shame.

The first time shame is mentioned in Scripture is after God created Adam and Eve. The Bible says, "Adam and his wife were both naked, and they felt no shame" (Gen. 2:25, NIV). But when Adam and

Eve broke the commandment God gave them to not eat from the tree of the knowledge of good and evil, Genesis 3:7 says their eyes were opened. They immediately saw their nakedness, sewed fig leaves together to cover themselves, and hid.

> Then the LORD God called to Adam and said to him, "Where are you?"
> So he said, "I heard Your voice in the garden, and I was afraid because I was naked; and I hid myself."
> And He said, "Who told you that you were naked?"
> —GENESIS 3:9–11, NKJV

Shame was the first emotion felt after sin entered the world.

I have prayed for many people who have experienced shame. It's very debilitating. Shame can come in so many ways. Ultimately, shame is demonic. The enemy uses it to destroy your life, embarrassing and humiliating you. Listen to me. I want you to hear this. God does not want you to feel and experience shame or humiliation. Sometimes as I've dealt with people who have backslidden or fallen into sin—maybe unwanted pregnancy or something else they're ashamed of and they've repented for—I have had to minister deliverance. I've had to come against spirits of guilt, shame, and condemnation. Those are demons that work together.

Shame also comes if someone has been raped or sexually abused. Even though this person is the victim, he or she can experience shame and blame for what's been done to him or her. Years ago, I read *Maimed by Shame* by Win Worley. It's a deliverance book in which the author shows how shame can maim you. It can cause you to hang your head, to look down on yourself and lose self-respect and self-esteem. God did not create you for that. He created you to be a person of honor and respect, someone with good self-esteem. He doesn't want you to hate or reject yourself. Self-hatred and self-rejection are other demons I've dealt with when ministering deliverance to people who are dealing with shame.

Other aspects of shame show up in our lives if we're ashamed we haven't succeeded or done certain things. Some people get to a certain age and haven't accomplished what they had hoped to do. They look at someone else's life and compare themselves. Or they've made some bad decisions that have set them back. These kinds of experiences can cause a lot of heartbreak and hurt, leading to shame.

The good news is you can be delivered from shame. You can get your respect and honor back. Proverbs 4 tells us that wisdom brings honor. Wisdom will cause you to be promoted, respected, honored, and to have a good name. We should all have this desire.

WHAT IS SHAME?

When I began to write this chapter, I researched shame and found a couple of definitions. The first one, from *Merriam-Webster*, defines shame as "a painful emotion caused by consciousness of guilt, shortcoming, or impropriety; a condition of humiliating disgrace or disrepute; something that brings censure or reproach."[1] Another dictionary calls it "a painful feeling of humiliation or distress caused by the consciousness of wrong or foolish behavior."[2] Shame is painful. When you do something wrong or foolish, you're embarrassed.

Have you ever said, "I'm so embarrassed by what I said," "I'm so ashamed of what I did," "I shouldn't have done that," "That was stupid," "That was foolish," or "I feel so bad"? Those are the remorseful or regretful words connected to shame over foolish or wrong behavior. I've said things like this to people after saying something out of line. Sometimes we speak or act in foolish ways. We don't mean to behave that way, but sometimes things come out wrong. It can be embarrassing and even painful or humiliating to think of how our actions negatively affected something.

The key to defeating shame is a process of apologizing, repenting, and attempting to make things right. Wisdom leads us to do this. It's part of restoring honor. Don't let embarrassment fester. The longer you hold on to pride, the more deeply shame can grab hold of you. Apologize and make amends quickly. Set the record straight, admit your wrongs, and get back in good standing.

In the case of abuse or something you've experienced that leaves you feeling humiliated and disgraced, we'll talk about how to restore honor in this area a little bit later in this chapter.

But hear me now: Regardless of the cause, God does not want you to be shamed or disgraced. You were not born and put on the earth to walk in shame and disgrace. Wisdom comes in and says, "I'm going to teach you how to live your life so that you will not experience shame and disgrace. Instead, you will have respect, honor, and a good name." Wisdom teaches us how to conduct our lives in such a way that we avoid shame, embarrassment, and dishonor.

WHAT WISDOM TEACHES US ABOUT SHAME

God created you in His image and likeness. He does not want you to live with low self-esteem, shame, and embarrassment. Nor does He want you to do something so foolish that it brings disrepute into your life. God wants to honor you, bless you, and cause happiness to abound.

God wants you to be respected like Job was. When Job showed up at the city gate, everyone held their tongues because of the way Job lived his life. He was both wealthy and respected. You can read about it in Job

29. Even aged men stood up in his presence. (See Job 29:8–10.)

Just as athletes don't have to ask for applause (their stats records speak for them), honorable men and women don't have to tell people to respect them. If you have to ask for respect, take a look at how you're living your life, the decisions you're making. Because if you have to force people to respect you, there's a problem. Your character and wisdom should bring respect. Even a wise child or young person commands respect. Remember how Joseph was honored by Pharaoh for his wisdom to interpret dreams? Pharaoh made him second in command in Egypt. (See Genesis 41.) Daniel was promoted and honored by King Nebuchadnezzar because of his wisdom. The king found no one as wise as Daniel. He was wiser than all the magicians and sorcerers of the land. (See Daniel 1:20; 2:48.) Let's look at some specific sources of shame.

Foolishness brings shame.

"The wise shall inherit glory: but shame shall be the promotion of fools" (Prov. 3:35). Honor comes through wisdom, but dishonor and shame come when you ignore wisdom. Foolishness is the opposite of wisdom. A fool ignores wisdom. Fools say and do foolish things, bringing shame, disrepute, and dishonor on themselves. Hear me when I say God does not want that for you.

Arguing with mockers brings shame.

"Whoever corrects a mocker invites insults; whoever rebukes the wicked incurs abuse" (Prov. 9:7, NIV). In other words, you and I waste our time trying to rebuke and argue with scorners. Avoid getting into shame-inducing arguments. They won't hear your reproof. I get that you want to see others have what you have. But some people you simply cannot help because they don't want to be helped. Rebuking them only brings shame on yourself.

I resist arguing with skeptics and mockers. I always want to live my life with honor and respect. I always want to be an honorable man. I want to be an honorable father, honored by my children, my wife, and my loved ones. I never want to be dishonored. My guess is you want that too. Follow the Scripture and don't waste your time and energy arguing with the wicked.

Hypocrisy brings shame.

Jesus said the Pharisees were like whitewashed tombs—dead inside—because of their hypocrisy. How many leaders in the body of Christ have been disrespected because they have done things that led people to say, "I don't respect them because I know how they live"? People don't receive or listen to what hypocritical leaders say because they preach one thing and do another. Think about the number of church leaders you've heard or read about who have made foolish decisions, especially in the area of sexuality. Hypocrisy is one of the surest and straightest pathways to shame.

Laziness brings shame.

"He who gathers crops in summer is a prudent son, but he who sleeps during harvest is a disgraceful son" (Prov. 10:5, NIV). This verse connects shame with work and tells us that a person who is slow and lazy when it's time to work causes shame. If you're lazy and don't want to work, you bring shame on yourself. No one will honor and respect you. If all you do is lie around and sleep, you don't want to work. You don't want to gather the harvest. At that point, you want someone else to take care of you. Yet you want people to respect you. By now you know it doesn't work like that. Shame awaits anyone who is able to work but doesn't and yet expects respect. We were created and wired to work. In Genesis, God put Adam to work naming the animals. Scripture is clear that laziness (Proverbs 19:15 calls it "slothfulness") brings embarrassment, hunger, and shame.

Pride brings shame.

"When pride comes, then comes shame; but with the humble is wisdom" (Prov. 11:2, NKJV). The Bible tells us that pride—the opposite of humility—goes before destruction. Wisdom says, "Don't allow pride, arrogance, and haughtiness to come into your life, because you will end up ashamed. You'll end up doing or saying something in such a way that you bring shame, reproach, dishonor, embarrassment, and humiliation to your life." Wisdom says, "I don't want you to be full of humiliation. I want to honor and bless you."

I've taught quite a bit on this. Pride, arrogance, haughtiness, vanity, ego—these are terrible spirits, with pride being the worst demon. Pride and shame go hand in hand. Humility, though, connects to wisdom, which in turn connects to fear of the Lord. You cannot have pride and wisdom together. If you are prideful, you will have shame—no honor, respect, or promotion. I've seen many people who were going strong, and suddenly pride stealthily crept in, followed by foolish decisions that brought shame. See the cycle?

Humiliation, disgrace, and embarrassment are never God's will for you. God tells you to pray for and pursue wisdom. It is the principal thing. (See Proverbs 4:7.) Wisdom should be a life priority. It will help you avoid shame, destruction, and even premature death. Wisdom will tell you what to do *and* what not to do.

An uncontrolled temper brings shame.

"A fool's wrath is known at once, but a prudent man covers shame" (Prov. 12:16, NKJV). Scripture asserts that when we have no control over our temper, we are like a city broken down without walls (Prov. 25:28). In the Bible, a city without walls was vulnerable to its enemies. Self-control acts as protection from our enemy. No wonder it's one of the fruits of the Spirit (Gal. 5:22–23). The enemy will take advantage of a person who has no control over his or her emotions. An uncontrolled temper destroys marriages, careers, and relationships with children, siblings, and friends.

It causes you to act and speak without thinking, and ultimately it leads to shame and destruction.

Lying and wickedness bring shame.

"A righteous man hates lying: but a wicked man is loathsome and comes to shame" (Prov. 13:5, NKJV). What we see here is the destructive and blatant connection between lying and wickedness. In essence this proverb tells us that if you lie, you are wicked, and that a wicked liar will be brought to shame. Honor requires you to walk in honesty and integrity. You cannot lie and be wicked and expect honor and promotion to come into your life. You must lay aside wickedness, especially lying.

Shameful behavior repels favor.

"The king's favor is toward a wise servant, but his wrath is against him who causes shame" (Prov. 14:35, NKJV). Notice here that with wrath and shame comes judgment. The king judges between the two servants and is angry with the servant who caused shame. You cannot please the king, Jesus, if you're causing shame or doing shameful, embarrassing, or humiliating things with your life.

Shameful actions affect more than just you.

"A wise servant will rule over a son who causes shame and will share an inheritance among the brothers" (Prov. 17:2, NKJV). In other words, a wise servant who doesn't bring shame will eventually rule over a son who causes shame. This is interesting because sometimes people in our family can bring shame to the family. Our children or siblings, and sometimes our parents, can bring shame into our lives. We can be embarrassed by what they do. The enemy may try to use those in your life to invoke shame. Of course there is forgiveness, redemption, and mercy, but I've seen many parents struggle with shame, not because of their actions, but because of what their children or other family members have done.

You might say, "Well, my family's actions don't affect me." Yes, they do. And what you do affects your family. No one is an island. Someone may say, "Well, I'll do what I want to do. This is my life." You're right; it is your life. But you're connected to people. What you do does affect other people. So in wisdom, it would be irresponsible and shortsighted to have a reckless attitude that says, "It's my life. I do what I want to do. No one can tell me what to do." Often our behavior has a ripple effect. The consequences we face because of our actions do impact others. Your shameful actions can lead to a negative effect on loved ones, friends, and other relationships. Make sure you live your life with prudence and discretion so that you can be a blessing and bring honor to the people you're connected with.

Speaking too quickly brings shame.

"He who answers a matter before he hears it, it is folly and shame to him" (Prov. 18:13, NKJV). The admonition here is simple but so needed: don't thoughtlessly speak about something until you hear the matter, because answering too quickly can bring shame or embarrassment. You may find yourself saying something like, "Oh, I'm so sorry. I didn't know." No, you didn't know, because you didn't take time to seek out and investigate the whole matter. You spoke before you knew the whole situation. It's wiser to wait to act or to speak until you know the whole situation. You may not only bring shame or embarrassment, but you may also cause hurt and pain. Have you ever jumped to conclusions or judgment about a person and corroborated a story about them that got them in trouble? Maybe they were fired from a job or arrested. Maybe they were demoted from a place of favor or honor because of your testimony. When you discovered the whole truth about the person, you were ashamed or you felt guilty because of the pain or hurt you caused them.

Wisdom teaches us to slow down and take time to look at the whole matter. Sometimes we're so quick to speak that we don't search out all sides of the story. We hear one person's side, and we jump on it. Then when we finally listen to the other side, we realize how wrong we were and how quick we were to judge. Embarrassment can quickly turn to shame. What a word of wisdom this proverb offers!

Dishonoring your parents brings shame.

"He who mistreats his father and chases away his mother is a son who causes shame and brings reproach" (Prov. 19:26, NKJV). Wow. This verse connects shame to the way you treat your parents. Scripture clearly tells us that if you chase away your parents or mistreat them, you bring shame to yourself. So here we find shame mentioned in the context of the family. And again, what we do in family relationships can bring shame, embarrassment, and humiliation to the family. We don't want our family name to be dishonored. We want to protect it. When people hear your family's name, they shouldn't cringe with horror: "Yes, I know about them." While you might not be able to control what everyone in your family does, you can control what you say and do, and you can let everyone in your family know that what *they* do and say represents the family.

Wisdom teaches us that we should want to protect the honor of our fathers and mothers and their family name. Bringing our parents honor and respect helps us avoid shame.

Moving in haste—assuming what you don't know—can bring shame.

"Do not go hastily to court; for what will you do in the end, when your neighbor has put you to shame? (Prov. 25:8, NKJV). This is pretty easy to understand: don't be too quick to get into an argument or fight, because your enemy or your neighbor can put you to shame. They may embarrass you. Have you ever seen people who go around thinking they can whip anyone and then they get whipped? It's embarrassing. You avoid shame by staying out of fights and also by humbly approaching disagreements. Confidence is a good thing when it's kept in balance, but it's also wise not to underestimate other people.

Becoming famous for the wrong things brings shame.
"Debate your case with your neighbor, and do not disclose the secret to another; lest he who hears it expose your shame, and your reputation be ruined" (Prov. 25:9–10, NKJV). This verse presents its wisdom in the context of being legally taken to court, being put to shame, and becoming infamous as a result. We all know the word *infamy*, probably most famously delivered from President Roosevelt's lips on December 8, 1941. The attack of Pearl Harbor, he said, would live as a day of infamy. None of us wants to be famous for doing or saying the wrong thing. It only leads to shame.

Keeping bad company brings shame.
"Whoever keeps the law is a discerning son, but a companion of gluttons shames his father" (Prov. 28:7). The people you choose to spend your life with matter. They matter to you and to God. Scripture talks about our companions because God knows that your friends can lead you down the right or wrong path. Again, He doesn't want us to experience the debilitating emotion of shame, so He put safeguards in His Word to help us avoid it. Hanging out with the wrong crowd leads to shame for both you and your parents. As I mentioned above, you want to honor your father and mother by the way you live, walking in wisdom. We'll

talk more in chapter 10 about the role wise friends and connections have in restoring honor and rebuilding your life after loss.

A child who is not corrected brings shame.
"The rod and rebuke give wisdom, but a child left to himself brings shame to his mother" (Prov. 29:15, NKJV). If you don't correct a child and teach him the way to live, pouring wisdom into him, he will bring shame to both you and himself. He will end up living a life that breaks your heart and God's. You may be the child of a parent who didn't correct you, and now your life is showing the signs of his or her failure to discipline and set boundaries.

Whatever the situation, there is deliverance and restoration. Our lives do not have to remain in a shameful place. God is in the business of rebuilding and restoring us back to lives of honor and favor.

GET DELIVERED FROM SHAME

As we've explored in this chapter, I hope you can see that lack of wisdom in our lives leads to shame, which can cause tremendous pain, embarrassment, humiliation, and loss of favor, trust, and opportunity for promotion. Shame hurts. It hurts those around you. God does not want that kind of life for you. Instead He wants you to live a life filled with wisdom and honor. To get back what shame steals, sometimes we need deliverance. Even if you're not the one directly responsible for your feelings of shame, dishonor, or disrespect, you can still be freed. You don't have to be maimed by shame. Let's pray now so the Holy Spirit can begin the process of delivering you from shame and restoring you to a place of honor.

PRAYER OF DELIVERANCE FROM SHAME

Father, I pray that You deliver me from shame. Lord, I don't want shame and humiliation to be a part of my life. Lord, I ask for wisdom so that I may walk in honor, respect, and promotion. I believe that wisdom brings honor, and that You want to honor me. I believe that You want to give me a crown of glory and a crown of honor. I believe that You do not want me to experience shame, hurt, pain, embarrassment, humiliation, dishonor, and reproach.

So Father, I pray that I will walk in wisdom, discretion, prudence, knowledge, and understanding all the days of my life. Lord, let me not do or say anything that brings shame, embarrassment, and humiliation to me or to my loved ones.

Wherever I have experienced personal shame, Lord, I pray for Your deliverance. In Your name, I come against the spirits of shame, condemnation, guilt, humiliation, dishonor, and reproach. I come against those spirits that try to torment me. I command them to go in the name of Jesus. I command spirits of low self-esteem, self-hatred, and self-rejection to go in the name of Jesus. I come against the spirit of pride, which also brings shame and embarrassment.

I ask You, Lord, to forgive me of any shameful relationships and things I've done in those relationships that I am ashamed of. Lord, release me from the shame I experience over the things I've done in the past. You said if anyone is in Christ, they are a new creation and the old things are passed away. You said, "Behold, all things have become new." I receive this word in my life.

Father, I thank You for Your forgiveness, redemption, and deliverance. As I have been one to walk around with my head down, feeling embarrassed about my life and my life choices, Lord, I pray now for wisdom to come. Let Your restoration come, O God. I pray for redemption to cover my sins so that I may be forgiven. Give me a new start in life. Let me walk in wisdom and not do anything that brings shame. Let my name be a good name. Let my family have a good name. Keep me from doing anything shameful that would embarrass my church or ministry, my pastors, or my loved ones. Help *me to know the importance of my lifestyle and my decisions.*

Bring honor, glory, and promotion to my life. Bless me. Let the blessings of wisdom come upon me as I learn its ways. All this I pray in Jesus' name. Amen

THE WORD OF THE LORD TO YOU CONCERNING HONOR

The Lord said:

This is a time in which I'm reminding My people to value wisdom, for some have not made wisdom their priority, but as you prioritize wisdom and as you desire wisdom, I'm pouring a spirit of wisdom upon you. I'm putting a new spirit of wisdom into your life. I'm going to cause you to walk in a realm of wisdom. This is the day in which I'm increasing My wisdom in your life.

Do not be satisfied with the level of wisdom you have. As you grow older, you will increase in wisdom each year. Believe Me for an increase in wisdom. You'll have more wisdom this year than you had last year. You'll have more wisdom next year than you do this year. I'm the God of increase. I'm the God who pours out more. I'm the God who gives you more.

I will crown you with glory and honor. I will cause My favor and blessing to come upon your life as you grow and increase in wisdom. Do not draw back, but hear My word of wisdom. Hear My instruction of wisdom. Receive understanding and knowledge. Walk in My fear and humility and watch My blessings of wisdom come upon your life. Watch honor and respect begin to come upon your life. Then you will know what it means to be happy and joyful. The sadness, grief, pain, and humiliation of shame will live far from you.

This is a new day, and I'm releasing My teaching on wisdom in this hour. I'm causing many of My servants to teach on the importance of wisdom. I'm anointing many of My teachers to share from the Word of God concerning wisdom.

You will be like Solomon. I gave him honor. I gave him glory. I gave him great respect throughout all the lands. Many came to him because of his great name. I gave him great honor, and I will honor you as well. I will promote you as well. I cause My favor, grace, prosperity, and blessing to come upon you.

I'm enlightening you and giving you understanding of this important subject as you study and learn about it. You will see the many facets and the many blessings that wisdom brings into your life. As you walk in these things, you will walk not only in My manifold wisdom, but you will also walk in My manifold blessing.

This is the day of wisdom. When My kingdom

comes, I bring wisdom. There's wisdom with My kingdom. There's wisdom with My Spirit, My Holy Spirit, the One who feels you, the One who inspires you, the One who leads you. As you walk in the Spirit, you're walking in wisdom, for He is the One who gives you counsel and wisdom. So be a person of the Spirit—living, walking, singing, and praying in Him. As you come to know what it means to walk in the power of wisdom, then blessing, favor, riches, and honor shall be your portion in the days to come.

I release this word to you today. I prophesy to you a new release of wisdom. Let the winds of wisdom blow upon you. Even if you have walked in foolishness in the past, repent and turn to wisdom. Renounce all foolishness. Anything that is contrary to God's wisdom, renounce it today. Turn away from it. Ask God to remove it from your life. Recommit today to walk in God's wisdom and to make it your priority in the months and years to come. Even as we close out this chapter, give God praise for what He is about to do in your life. Give Him glory and honor right now for His goodness, mercy, and the blessings of wisdom.

CHAPTER 8

GOODNESS AND GLORY

If ye then, being evil, know how to give good gifts unto your children, how much more shall your Father which is in heaven give good things to them that ask him?

—Matthew 7:11

Y<small>OU MAY BE</small> facing one of the worst seasons of your life. Things may not be lining up how you envisioned. You may be exhausted from the fight to remain faithful while your world is turned upside down. You may be battling shame, guilt, or discouragement from yesterday's losses. Well, I want to keep you encouraged and believing God for good things. Things will turn around. You shall recover all. God is setting you up for the greatest comeback, the greatest turnaround you've ever experienced. He will restore to you what the locusts have eaten. Joy, wholeness, abundance, and peace will be yours again.

I want to encourage you to continue to press into God and make your requests known to Him. Ask and keep asking. The Bible says that when you ask Him, He will give you good things. He will even give you things you didn't ask for. God is able to do exceedingly abundantly above all that you ask or think (Eph. 3:20). Seek first His kingdom and His righteousness, and all these things will be added unto you (Matt. 6:33). What He gives you is not limited to what you're asking for. God wants to go beyond that and give you more than what you asked for. That's the goodness of God we're going to talk about—His glory and good things and how they are connected.

In the Book of Exodus when Moses asked God to show him His glory, the Lord responded, saying: "I will make all my goodness pass before thee" (Exod. 33:19). So God equates goodness with glory. His glory is His goodness. And God's goodness is His mercy and lovingkindness. This means that when you begin to move in the glory realm, you'll also begin to tap into the goodness realm. Good things come through God's glory.

Now, I've preached and written a lot on the subject of glory. Glory brings favor. I call Isaiah 60 the glory chapter. It is a whole list of good things that come through God's glory. We'll take a look at this in just a minute.

As I wrote in my book *The Good Land*, Psalm 37:11 tells us that the meek shall inherit the earth, or the land, and enjoy peace and prosperity. Matthew 5:5 points back to Psalm 37:11. When Psalm 37:11 talks about "earth," it is talking about the land of Canaan, or Israel.[1] The natural land of Israel—Canaan, or the Promised Land—is a type and symbol of the kingdom, living in Christ, or living in the kingdom of God. It is a symbol of good land that yields good things—the land of milk and honey. Spiritually, this is the land God wants you to live in. He wants you to enjoy the good things of the good land.

GOOD THINGS ACCOMPANY GOD'S GLORY

Getting back to Isaiah 60, we see how Scripture talks about what happens when the glory of God comes upon you:

> Arise, shine, for your light has come, and the glory of the Lord rises upon you. See, darkness covers the earth and thick darkness is over the peoples, but the Lord rises upon you and his glory appears over you. Nations will come to your light, and kings to the brightness of your dawn.
> Lift up your eyes and look about you: All assemble and come to you; your sons come from afar, and your daughters are carried on the hip.
> —Isaiah 60:1–4, niv

God will give you good children and good things. Children are the heritage of the Lord, both naturally and spiritually. Children are "good things."

> Then you will look and be radiant, your heart will throb and swell with joy; the wealth on the seas will be brought to you, to you the riches of the nations will come.
>
> —Isaiah 60:5, niv

Notice that the good things are connected to glory. Good things and glory go together.

> Herds of camels will cover your land, young camels of Midian and Ephah. And all from Sheba will come, bearing gold and incense and proclaiming the praise of the Lord.
> All Kedar's flocks will be gathered to you, the rams of Nebaioth will serve you; they will be accepted as offerings on my altar, and I will adorn my glorious temple.
>
> —Isaiah 60:6–7, niv

So God begins to talk about all these good things that come because of God's glory.

> Foreigners will rebuild your walls, and their kings will serve you. Though in anger I struck you, in favor I will show you compassion.
>
> —Isaiah 60:10, niv

I love glory because it brings favor, and favor is a good thing. When you get in glory, you worship in glory and you experience the presence, beauty, glory, and splendor of the Lord. There are good things connected to that. I recommend going to a church that is full of glory. Don't go to a dead church where there's no presence and no glory. Get around the glory of God.

> Your gates will always stand open, they will never be shut, day or night, so that people may bring you the wealth of the nations.
> —Isaiah 60:11, niv

Wealth comes through glory. In Haggai 2:7–8 God says, "'I will fill this house with glory....The silver is mine and the gold is mine,' declares the Lord Almighty" (niv). This verse shows us that gold and silver, wealth and riches are connected to glory. Good things are connected to glory.

Isaiah 60 tells you that your life will be rebuilt when glory comes. Your walls will be rebuilt. Glory opens us up to a time of restoration—a good thing you may need most in this season. When glory comes, restoration comes. God restores and heals you. That is a good thing. As I talk about good things, I'm not just talking about material things. I'm talking about the spiritual things of salvation, restoration, power, influence, favor, and promotion. Those are all good things that are connected with the glory of God.

THE GLORY REALM IS A REALM OF GOD'S GOODNESS

As I mentioned above, when Moses asked God to show him His glory, God said that He would cause His goodness to pass before Moses. God equates His goodness with His glory. Scripture says the earth shall be filled with the knowledge of the glory of the Lord as the waters cover the sea (Hab. 2:14). So you can see it this way: the earth shall be filled with the glory of the good things of the Lord—salvation, deliverance, healing, restoration, wealth, prosperity, and favor. Every place shall be filled with the glory of good things of the Lord as the waters cover the sea. God wants the earth to be filled with His blessings and good things.

Salvation is a part of your coming into the glory realm: Christ in you, the hope of glory (Col. 1:27). The Spirit of God is the glory of God within you. When you feel the Spirit of God, glory comes into your life. When the anointing is on your life, glory rests upon you. Glory and the Spirit are connected. In fact, the Spirit of God is called the Spirit of glory (1 Pet. 4:14), Jesus is called the Lord of glory (1 Cor. 2:8), and the Father is called the Father of glory (Eph. 1:17).

HOW GOOD THINGS COME

1. A good relationship with God—When you have relationship with the Father, He meets all of your needs according to His

riches in glory (Phil. 4:19). Glory is full of riches, and all your needs are met.

2. Giving—Good things also come as a result of giving. Giving can release good things to you. "Give, and it shall be given unto you; good measure, pressed down, and shaken together, and running over" (Luke 6:38).

3. Dwelling in the glory realm—Good things begin to come your way when you get around the glory and presence of God by going to a church full of glory, getting around ministers who carry glory, worshipping in the glory, and living in the glory realm.

4. Ask God—God has many ways of getting good things into your life. You can ask for good things, and you shall not lack any good thing. God is able to do exceedingly abundantly above all you ask or think (Eph. 3:20).

5. Remain upright, righteous, and holy—God says that the upright shall always have good things: "no good thing will he withhold from them that walk uprightly" (Ps. 84:11).

6. Seek God and His kingdom—When you seek God and His kingdom and righteousness first, all good things will be added to you (Matt. 6:33).

7. Do good to others—Galatians 6:6 says, "Let him who is taught the word share in all good things with him who teaches" (NKJV). You can give good things to your leaders, pastors, and ministers, and God will reciprocate that generosity by giving you good things. The next verse tells us, "Do not be deceived, God is not mocked; for whatever a man sows, that he will also reap" (Gal. 6:7, NKJV). You can receive good things through sowing and reaping. By doing good things for other people, God will cause you to reap good things.

8. Speak good things—By allowing good things to come out of your mouth, good things can come to you. "A good man out of the good treasure of his heart brings forth good; and an evil man out of the evil treasure of his heart brings forth evil. For out of the abundance of the heart his mouth speaks" (Luke 6:45, NKJV).

9. Confession—God creates the fruit of the lips, so good things come through

confession through the prophetic word. The prophetic word releases good things. As you prophesy, or as someone prophesies to you, good things can begin to happen because the word of the Lord releases good things.

Because God's glory dwells within our hearts, you will have good relationships, good children, good platforms, good doors of opportunity, good success, good health, good places to live, good cars to drive, good houses to live in, good vacations, good things, good clothes, good shoes, good finances, and good business. God wants to give you good things.

When you ask to see God's glory, He will cause His goodness to pass before you just as He did for Moses. And when His goodness passes before you, you'll begin to see good things happen in your life.

No matter what you've experienced in the past or how many bad things have happened to you, I want you to believe God for good things to come in your life now and in the days to come. You shall recover all. I want you to believe good things are coming. Confess it and ask for it. Seek God. Walk uprightly. Believe that God will do it for you. He is a good, good God, and His goodness is abundant. There's no limit to the good things you can have. Lay aside those bad things, those bad experiences, and believe God for good experiences, good encounters, good manifestations, and good favor. Trust that God wants to give you good things.

I invite you to pray these prayers and speak these confessions and decrees as you believe God for good things.

PRAYER FOR GOOD THINGS

Heavenly Father, I am Your child, and I ask You for good things. I believe I will receive good things in my life. I believe You will withhold no good thing from me. I will not lack any good thing. Open Your treasury in heaven and release good things in my life. Let my house be filled with good things. Let my days be filled with good things. Let my ears be filled with good things.

I reject every bad thing sent by the enemy into my life. Father, You are abundant in goodness. Let me be filled with abundance. Let me live in the good land and enjoy good things. Father, I believe You take pleasure in giving me good things. In Jesus' name, I pray. Amen.

CONFESSIONS FOR GOOD THINGS

- I will have good relationships.
- I will have good seasons.

- I will have good nights.
- I will have good resources.
- I will have good finances.
- I will have good wealth and riches.
- I will speak and confess good things.
- I will have good rest.
- I will have good health.
- I will have good success.
- I will have good strategies.
- I will have good counsel and good advice.
- I will make good decisions.
- I will walk good paths.
- I will enjoy good things.
- I will walk through good doors.
- I will have good connections.
- I will have good ministers minister to me.
- I will be a part of a good church.
- I will have good business.
- I will have good transportation.
- I will have good vacations.
- I will eat good things.

- I will have good dreams.
- I will experience good worship.
- I will sing good songs.
- I will have good gifts.
- I will receive good words.
- I will have good favor.
- I will have good promotions.
- I will receive good reports.
- I will hear good news.
- I will have good harvests.
- I will receive good surprises.
- I will receive good benefits.
- I will inherit the good land.
- I will experience good breakthroughs, and goodness and mercy will follow me all the days of my life.
- I will praise the Lord for the good things He gives me and the good things He does in my life.
- Let anything in my life hindering good things from coming to me be exposed and removed from my life: pride, dis-obedience, sin, rebellion, bitterness, unforgiveness, fear, doubt, unbelief, bad

relationships, bad soul ties. Lord, let these things be exposed and removed from my life.

WORD OF THE LORD TO YOU CONCERNING GOOD THINGS

The Lord says:

I am a God of abundance. I'm abundant in goodness, and I've come to give you a greater revelation of My goodness and good things. I've come to increase your faith. I've come to stir you up. I've come to challenge you to believe Me for more. Walk in faith, for I desire to release more good things to you who have suffered at the hands of the enemy.

I'm delivering you out of captivity. I am bringing you out of the bad land, from the place of captivity called Egypt, and into the good land. I take you through the wilderness, and I bring you into the good land where you will enjoy My good things.

This is the day to cross over and move into the good things. I've ordained it for you to come into the land of milk and honey. As you get revelation and understand it, begin to confess it, begin to pray it, begin to believe it, and begin to expect it.

I'm going to release even greater things in your life, and you will experience good things.

This release will cause great praise, great worship, and great joy to be a part of your life. I'm going to break the cycle of bad things that have happened to you and the works of darkness that have come, and I'm going to give you the shield of faith, whereby you will stand against every attack of hell. When the enemy sends bad things your way, you will reverse and rebuke them. You will come against them with power and authority, and you'll see My goodness in the land of the living.

You will not have to wait until you go to heaven to experience My goodness. You will experience My goodness in the land of the living in the day in which you now live. You will experience My goodness, My light, My glory, and My splendor; and My blessing shall come upon you.

Even as you seek to walk in My glory and enjoy My presence, My beauty, and My splendor in worship...as you allow the Spirit of glory even to rest in your assembly...as you allow glory to come in your assemblies, allow My glory to rest there, and as you become a glory carrier and a glory chaser, watch as My goodness begins to manifest in your life.

You will reap the reward of glory and goodness. Truly, Isaiah 60 shall be your portion—for wealth and riches, sons and daughters, restoration and favor shall be your portion. You will rise and shine for My glory has come and risen upon you. So rise, shine, and be full of My glory.

Then watch as wealth, riches, finances, favor, restoration, and breakthrough dwell in your land. One thousandfold increase and multiplication shall come.

I'll do good things for you, and you shall rejoice and be glad. You will confess and tell people about the goodness of the Lord. My goodness will cause them to repent. Oh, My goodness will cause people to come to Me. My goodness will cause people to be drawn to Me when they see My goodness in your life. They will say, "How can I enjoy this goodness?" and you will point them to Me.

When people see that I am good, merciful, and kind, and that My mercy endures forever to every generation, they will know the lovingkindness, tender mercy, grace, and favor of the Lord. So receive My goodness to use as your living testimony, and then others who are in darkness will see your life and My glory and goodness.

Even as the word of the Lord comes, this prophetic word comes to release you from the bad and bring you into the good. Even as the prophetic winds and the winds of goodness blow in your direction, there will be a change. There will be a shift in your life, and you will come into a place of goodness, a place of prosperity, a place of blessing, a place of renewal, and a place of restoration. Truly, good things shall be your portion in the days to come, and God's goodness shall rest strongly upon your life. I release it now, in Jesus' name.

CHAPTER 9

HOPE AGAINST HOPE

[Abraham,] who against hope believed in hope, that he might become the father of many nations, according to that which was spoken, so shall thy seed be.

—ROMANS 4:18

"I T IS SAD," the Scriptures say, "when you don't get what you hoped for. But when wishes come true, it's like eating fruit from the tree of life" (Prov. 13:12, ICB). In chapter 2 we looked at *The Message* translation of the same verse, but let's look at it again:

> Unrelenting disappointment leaves you heartsick,
> but a sudden good break can turn life around.
> —PROVERBS 13:12, MSG

I like that—a sudden break, a sudden turn. The Passion Translation says it this way: "When hope's dream seems to drag on and on, the delay can be depressing. But when at last your dream comes true, life's sweetness will satisfy your soul."

We hear a lot of teaching on faith and love, but very seldom do we hear teaching on the subject of hope. "And now abide faith, hope, love, these three; but the greatest of these is love" (1 Cor. 13:13, NKJV). We don't often deal with the subject of hope, but hope is very important. Hope is your dream. It's what you're believing for and looking forward to. It's something you're hoping will happen in your life.

The apostle Paul defined hope as the "confident expectation of good." (See 2 Corinthians 1:7, AMPC.) Hope is about what you're expecting—a dream, vision, or desire. You don't have it now, but you're hoping for it to manifest. All of us have hopes, whether they're related to our family, children, marriage, ministry, career success, finances, health, or whatever it is. We not only have hopes, but we're also hoping for something good. No one hopes for something bad. We hope for something good, something better, something that will be a blessing to us or someone else. As the confident expectation of good, hope is based on believing God's promises. There is no consistent, strong faith apart from having a living hope in our hearts—for faith is the substance of things hoped for (Heb. 11:1).

We should not only be hopeful but also "abound in hope." Notice this verse, Romans 15:13: "Now the God of hope fill you with all joy and peace in believing, that ye may abound in hope, through the power of the Holy Ghost." The Holy Spirit gives us the ability to abound in hope, not just to have hope. Through Him we have the ability to have more than enough hope. Your hope should not be small. The Spirit of God will give you the ability to abound in hope.

HOPE FOR NOW, HOPE FOR THE FUTURE

I want to pause a minute and tell you why I am writing this chapter in particular. How this teaching came about is important because it highlights where many believers are in their hearts when it comes to believing and hoping for the best. At the height of the COVID-19 pandemic and all the political upheaval, the fires, the hurricanes, and the breakdowns in certain communities within the body of Christ, someone came to me and asked, "Do you think all this is the fulfillment of the Book of Revelation?" My answer was this: "I really believe in the days to come. I believe that we're going to see great breakthroughs, great revival, and great glory. Even in the midst of what the world is going through at the time of this writing—a time in which things look bad—I believe great things are coming."

My words visibly shocked him. He told me, "You're a very rare preacher, because most preachers are teaching that this is the end, that this is the beginning of the Book of Revelation."

It is true that I don't preach the last days like most preachers do. My vision as a prophetic person, even though I'm a realist and know things can go bad, centers on what the Bible says the prophetic word comes to do: exhort, encourage, edify, and build us up. I'm not saying we just prophesy good things, but God has given us some tremendous promises through the prophetic word about glory and revival breakthrough. Many of us have received personal prophecies, and God has spoken some great things to us. One of the reasons why the prophetic ministry is so powerful is because the prophetic word gives you hope. It encourages and edifies you. It strengthens you.

Again, I do not believe that every time you get a prophetic word it must be something sweet and nice. God can correct and adjust you through His prophetic word. Still, the primary function of the prophetic word is what Paul says: "He who prophesies speaks edification and exhortation and comfort to men" (1 Cor. 14:3, NKJV). The prophetic word does bring hope. God is a God of hope.

The person then said to me, "Well, you're one of the few who's not teaching that everything's about to fall apart, the world is coming to an end, and bad days are coming."

While there are difficult times in life, and the beginning of the 2020 decade was a landmark season of difficulty for many the world over, I still believe the kingdom is here and increasing and that the glory of God is coming in greater measure than we've ever experienced before. "Of the increase of his government and peace," Isaiah 9:7 says, "there shall be no end" (NKJV). The latter glory will be greater than the former (Hag. 2:9). So we have every reason to hope and believe for good things ahead, that our best days are yet to come.

God reassures us in His Word that we can and should hope, that we need hope. I've heard people predict the end of the world and the last days since I got saved in 1978. Every time there's a news event, the end-times prophecy teachers come up with all these scenarios—whether they're blood moons or something else about Israel—about how everything is coming to an end, leaving everyone who hears them feeling pessimistic, sad, and depressed.

In most cases like this, however, people find hope in the rapture. Their hope is in the belief that they are getting out of here. Even as they see things falling apart, they place their hope in being rescued. Here we are preaching, teaching, prophesying, believing God, praying, and exercising dominion, yet we see everything as falling apart. We're going to rise up and take authority, while at the same time we're preaching or being taught that everything is falling apart. It's a double-minded message, and God is not the author of confusion. The Bible says, "A double minded man is unstable in all of his ways" (Jas. 1:8).

The church is sending out conflicting messages, and

people don't know what to believe. One day the message is positive and hopeful. The next day it's "Take cover—the world is ending!" If the message is that there is no hope and the world is falling apart, what are we praying for? What are we believing God for? There is no hope in that scenario. And yes, there's the vision of just being able to escape and go to heaven, but what hope can we have for the earth, for the planet? The Bible says the meek shall inherit the earth, but who wants it?

Yet there is a hope we should have in the victorious and triumphant God whose promises are yes and amen to those who are in Christ. We must hold on to the hope that Jesus came so that we would have life and have it more abundantly in the here and now (John 10:10), that we reign and sit with Him in heavenly places even now. We can believe we are overcomers now. We can believe that the meek inherit the earth now, that the glory of God's kingdom is increasing and expanding on earth now. The hope of salvation, deliverance, restoration, and *shalom* is for us now.

THE SPIRIT OF DELAY

My conversation with this person was good because it caused me to expand my thinking about Proverbs 13:12, which focuses on deferred hope. What this means to me is that while we can have hope for good things now, there is the reality of delay. Hope deferred makes the heart sick. If you have a dream, a vision, or a hope, if you are believing for something and there's a delay, it's emotionally and even spiritually difficult. The result of delayed hope can be heartsickness, which is the open door to hopelessness, despair, depression, sadness, and discouragement.

I've seen people become so hopeless and discouraged because it seems like none of their dreams come true. There's always a delay. I've heard people say, "I never seem to get a break in life," "Things never seem to turn for my good," or "Just when it seems like I'm about to get a breakthrough, everything falls apart. I am so depressed. I am so discouraged."

God is the God of hope, but He doesn't give you hope to defer it. He doesn't give you hope so you can lose hope. God doesn't play games with us. He doesn't give us a promise just to deny it. Sometimes I believe delay is the enemy. I believe that demons are trying to stop our dreams from coming to pass. Demons want you to become discouraged and frustrated. Later in this chapter we're going to pray against demonic delay and take authority over it. You can then take this model and take authority over any demonic spirits of delay working against your dreams and visions.

BREAKING THE SPIRIT OF DELAY

In Daniel 10 we learn about a war in the heavenlies that delayed the answer for Daniel's fervent prayers for the Hebrew people. For twenty-one days an angel was held back, and Daniel had to wait and continue to pray and fast. Satan was hindering the answer to his prayers. In this chapter God shows us through His Word that demons can try to stop and hinder the blessing of God, which is why we need to use our faith. We need to pray. If we have to fast for breakthrough like Daniel did, we need to do it. We need to take authority over every demonic hindrance, every demonic delay that comes against our finances, ministries, careers, or whatever we are believing God for. We must pray toward a manifestation and fulfillment.

As we take authority and pray in faith for our dreams to manifest, we combat hopelessness. To be hopeless is to be disappointed, discouraged, and in despair. It can even lead to suicide, depression, sadness, and sorrow. When people are hopeless, they give up. They lose hope. They say, "It will never happen," "I'm tired of fighting," "I'm tired of believing," and "I never seem to get a breakthrough."

If this sounds like you and you're depressed, discouraged, and frustrated, I don't want your heart to be sick. I want you to exercise your faith today and believe God that He gives us the desires of our hearts. Yes, hope deferred makes the heart sick, but when the desire comes, it is like a tree of life. A fulfilled desire makes life worth living. No one wants to live a life where nothing good ever happens, where it seems they never get a break.

Maybe you're doing everything you know to do—giving, praying, worshipping, and decreeing—but you never seem to get a breakthrough. Well today, right now, we take authority over every demonic spirit and every demonic hindrance that has been assigned against you—whether it's witchcraft or demonic attack trying to delay and deny your breakthrough. I'm believing God for supernatural breakthroughs. And when the desire comes, it will be like a tree of life for you. God wants you to enjoy life. As I said above, Jesus said, "I come that you might have life and have it more abundantly." (See John 10:10.)

Fasting for breakthrough

In looking at Daniel's story, we discover that fasting brings breakthrough. Daniel went on a fast. He did not eat any pleasant food for three weeks as he prayed. The Bible reveals that there was something happening in the heavens. The prince of Persia, a demonic principality, was fighting an angel. Finally, Michael the archangel got involved and opened the way for that angel to come and bring the answer to Daniel's prayers.

Fasting is good for breakthrough because you can use it against the enemy. When you fast, you humble yourself and believe God for breakthrough. You come against demonic hindrance and those spirits that are trying to stop and hinder you from receiving your hope, your dream, your vision, or what you're believing God for. I encourage you to get my book *Fasting for Breakthrough and Deliverance*. It's a revelation that God gave me on fasting.

Early in my ministry, we were taught to fast, but we

didn't really have a lot of revelation on it. We just did it. We quipped things like, "If you don't fast, you won't last." Then the Lord began to show me the power of fasting from scriptures I'd never even connected with fasting.

In difficult cases, when you know there's demonic interference and hindrances against you, fasting is very powerful. Fasting will keep you focused and centered on God's power instead of your own. Fasting keeps you aware of spiritual realities so that you have something to hold on to rather than getting discouraged, depressed, sad, and disappointed. Fasting will keep your flesh submitted and your spirit man elevated so you won't want to give up, backslide, and leave God. Fasting gives you the spiritual strength to rise up like Jesus did during His forty-day fast and rebuke the devil. (See Matthew 4:1–12, Mark 1:12–13, and Luke 4:1–13.) You will have the strength to rise up and say, "The devil is a liar."

Let's do this now. Use your authority and speak the following declarations:

- I come against every demonic delay, interference, or opposition in my life hindering the breakthroughs I am believing God for.

- I come against spirits that have been assigned to block, hinder, or obstruct me from seeing the manifestation of my dreams and visions coming to pass.

- Whether it's business, finances, health, relationships, ministry, career, house, property, or anything else, I bind and rebuke the demonic influences hindering God's blessing.

Sowing for breakthrough

Maybe you have experienced great opposition in your finances. You can't seem to get financial breakthrough. I believe that sowing and giving are ways you can break delays in that area. I encourage people to sow because I have experienced its power in my own life. Sowing can bring breakthrough in the certain realms when we sow in faith. The Bible says, "Give, and it shall be given unto you; good measure, pressed down, and shaken together, and running over" (Luke 6:38). Then, "He who sows sparingly will also reap sparingly; and he who sows bountifully will also reap bountifully" (2 Cor. 9:6, NKJV).

When you join these promises with fasting and prayer and decree that no demon or demonic interference will stop you, you'll begin to see amazing breakthrough. If it's witchcraft, sorcery, or divination, or you feel like there's some invisible force stopping you, then fasting, prophetic decrees, and sometimes a prophetic word can bring breakthrough and release so that your desire can come. Prophecy can bring deliverance: "He sent his word, and healed them, and delivered them from their destructions" (Ps. 107:20, NKJV).

DEVELOP STRONG FAITH

So we have all these weapons—the Word, confession, decrees, prophecy, fasting, faith—and then we find where the Scriptures say, "[Abraham] [w]ho against hope believed in hope" (Rom. 4:18). Abraham was strong in faith, yet he had a dream or desire that took many years to manifest. He wanted a son. When it looked like having a child was impossible, he believed in hope. Strong faith can bring breakthrough. Abraham was not weak in faith. Likewise, we cannot afford to be weak in faith. Let me say that again: if you want breakthroughs against strong demons, you cannot be weak in faith.

Remember when the disciples could not cast a certain demon out? (See Matthew 17:14–21.) They asked Jesus, "Lord, why could we not cast him out?" (v. 19). Jesus said, "Because of your unbelief" (v. 20). They didn't have strong faith. So you must develop your faith. Hear the Word of God, which is the word of faith. Get it in your heart. The Bible says, "The word is nigh thee, even in thy mouth, and in thy heart: that is, the word of faith" (Rom. 10:8). Confess the Word. Read the Word. Get strong in faith.

Against all hope, when it looked hopeless, Abraham still believed and he still hoped. If you're in a seemingly hopeless situation—on the verge of being depressed, discouraged, or disappointed—then work on growing your faith. You may have to do some fasting. Get the prophetic word in your life. You can stand against these delays and hindrances of the enemy. You don't have to be a victim of demonic interference.

I decree that this will be the season of breakthrough for your life: financial breakthrough, relationship breakthrough, ministry breakthrough, career breakthrough, and breakthroughs in your health. Will you believe in God for that too? If these demonic spirits have been assigned to you—spirits of delay, denial, hindrance, lack, blockage, and obstruction—I rebuke them in the name of Jesus. I come against them and drive them out. I decree that your desires will come. Begin to decree this on your own behalf:

- The desires of my heart will come.
- My hope will not be deferred.
- My heart will not be sick.
- I will not be disappointed.
- I will not be discouraged, frustrated, depressed, sad, or disappointed.
- I will eat from the tree of life.
- My hope will manifest, and it will not tarry.
- My dreams and my visions will come to pass.
- I will see it happen.

GET REINFORCEMENT

Of course, there are dreams and goals that take time to happen. As you take up the fight, don't allow yourself to be weak in faith and get discouraged to the point of giving up. Ask someone to pray for you. Go to the leaders in your church or a mature and prophetic person in the Spirit. Ask them to lay hands on you and give you a prophetic word. Sometimes we keep so much to ourselves, thinking we should be mature enough to face great discouragement and difficulty alone. We are not. This is why we have the church. It is a fellowship of believers we can lean on, where we can bear each other's burdens.

When is the last time you received prophetic ministry? Don't say it's been years. Man or woman of God, we are prophetic people. Get to someone who can deliver the word of the Lord to you. Let God speak to you through them. God can and will speak into your situation. And sometimes in the midst of the prophetic word, the word of the Lord comes to rebuke delay, denial, and demonic interference and hindrances. This happened in Zechariah 3 when the prophet saw Satan standing at the right hand of Joshua the high priest. The enemy had come to resist him, and the Lord said, "The LORD rebuke thee, O Satan" (v. 2).

Let the rebuke of the Lord come against every demonic spirit that comes to disappoint and cast you down. Let the rebuke of the Lord come against every demonic spirit that comes to make you depressed and cause you to give up. The Lord rebuke every demonic spirit that causes you to be disappointed and sad. The Lord rebuke every demonic spirit that causes you to lose.

BE STRONG AND DON'T GIVE UP

I pray that you will be encouraged today, that you will be stirred and lifted up. I pray that the answers to your prayers, hopes, and dreams manifest. I pray that breakthroughs come during this season so you won't feel hopeless.

Hopelessness is one of the worst conditions you can be in. When a person becomes hopeless, they can get to a place where they want to give up. They become so exhausted by the fight that they can become suicidal. They can go into a pit, a place of despair. This is not God's will. You cannot enjoy life if you're hopeless, disappointed, and overcome by the spirit of heaviness.

If you are tired and feeling hopeless, again, reach out to someone such as your pastor, a prophetic minister, or a counselor. Even now, I pray for joy. I pray that the joy of the Lord will be your strength. I pray you will hold on. Joy manifests when your desire comes. You can enjoy the benefits of your dreams and your visions coming to pass.

As much as you can lean on God's power, don't allow the enemy to stop the will of God from happening in your life. Be strong and come against demons of blockage, obstruction, delay, witchcraft—whatever is coming against you to stop you. Because when you stop believing, you stop hoping, you stop trusting, and you give up.

You cannot afford to be hopeless. You need hope. Faith is the substance of things hoped for. If you have no hope, your faith has nothing to work on. This is not the season to give up. Believe God. I know it's been a long battle and you've been believing God. But if it seems like you're mired in a pit and can't come out, I rebuke the enemy and say you are coming out of that dark place. You are coming out of that prison of despair, discouragement, and despondency. Heaviness, darkness, gloominess, sadness, and depression—I rebuke all of it.

If you've opened the door for those spirits to come in because of what you've gone through and because it feels like nothing seems to happen—or if you've said things like, "I guess it'll never happen. Nothing ever goes my way"—I break the power of those words, those self-inflicted curses, in the name of Jesus. I rebuke them, and I pray for the word of the Lord to manifest in your life.

MAY YOUR DREAMS COME FORTH

You are coming out of this. Just as Jesus said, "Roll the stone away," before He raised Lazarus from the dead, He is saying this to you today. Roll away the stone, because you are coming out of that tomb. Lazarus had been dead for four days, but Jesus spoke and Lazarus came forth.

I speak to your dead dreams, visions, and hopes and say, "Come forth." They may have died days, months, or years ago, but in the name of Jesus I call out to those dreams, "Come forth!" And to you I say, "Come out of that hole. Come out of that place of darkness, despair, death, and destruction, and live again. Take off those graveclothes and live again, breathe again, and have joy again."

Pray this prayer with me now.

PRAYER FOR HOPE TO BE MANIFESTED

Father, I pray and I believe You for great breakthroughs so that I will not experience deferred hope—so that my heart will not be sick, and I will not be depressed, discouraged, frustrated, ready to give up, suicidal, heavy, or sad. I decree that I will eat from the tree of life, that my desires will come and they will be like a tree of life to me.

Father, I decree that my hope will manifest and the tree of life will be my portion. I decree that delay will be broken and denial will not be my portion. I come against the spirits of denial, delay, obstruction, blockage, resistance, and demonic interference that would come to hinder my dreams, visions, and hopes. I pray that the angels of God would come on my behalf as they did for Daniel and break through for me so that I will receive the answers to my prayers.

Lord, as I believe You for financial health; spiritual, mental, and emotional health; my relationships, business, or ministry, I pray that this will be a season of restoration and fulfillment, that I will not only have hope, but that I will abound in hope. I will not be hopeless or given over to disappointment. I will not be overcome by despair and discouragement. Instead, I will be full of hope. I will be strong in faith. I decree this and believe it now. In Jesus' name, amen.

Be encouraged. If you've been wading through this season in despair, shake yourself loose. Arise from the dust. Come from that low place. Rise up and enjoy the promises of God. Know that what God said, He will watch over it to perform it. He cannot and will not lie. He will perform it for you.

CHAPTER 10

GET YOUR EDGE BACK

As iron sharpens iron, so a man sharpens the countenance of his friend.
—Proverbs 27:17, NKJV

Proverbs 27:17 is a verse of Scripture you've probably heard and know well, but I want to look at it in depth and challenge us to dig deeper. It's a proverb, yes, and you may recall that the Book of Proverbs is also known as the Book of Wisdom. And wisdom, as we know by now, is the key to living a good, competent, and prosperous life. Wisdom keeps you from making a mess of your life. It keeps you from making mistake after mistake. Even when life is difficult and it seems like one bad thing after another is coming, wisdom will help you navigate safely through the storms of life.

This verse has an interesting phrase, especially

as the Hebrew is translated in the New King James Version. It says, "...so a man sharpens the countenance of his friend." By using the word *friend*, we can see that this verse is talking about friendship and relationship. Choosing the right friends is one of the most important things in life. You show me someone's friends, and I'll show you his or her future. Looking at someone's friends, I can predict whether he or she is going to fail or succeed. You choose the right friends, because that choice is a part of wisdom's directive. Being with the wrong friends can damage and hurt your life. We need good friends.

Another verse says, "There is a friend that sticks closer than a brother" (Prov. 18:24, NKJV). That's a covenant friend. Sometimes it's hard to find a faithful friend: someone who's loyal and will not stab you in the back; someone who will not betray, deceive, or take advantage of you; and someone who will not use or manipulate you.

You may be reading this now and saying, "I don't have any friends." Well, you need good friends—good covenant friends. As bad friends destroy your life, good friends help you build and sustain a good life.

The other part of this verse I want to emphasize is the word *countenance*. Often when this verse is taught, the focus tends to stay on the "iron sharpens iron" part, but there's so much more to it. Until recently I really didn't pay as close attention to the second part of the verse.

When I looked up all the other scriptures on friendship, I saw that the word *friend* is mentioned eighteen times in the Book of Proverbs. Some of the verses are familiar, such as the following:

- "A friend loveth at all times, and a brother is born for adversity" (Prov. 17:17).

- "Many entreat the favor of the nobility, and every man is a friend to one who gives gifts" (Prov. 19:6, NKJV).

- "Make no friendship with an angry man, and with a furious man do not go, lest you learn his ways and set a snare for your soul" (Prov. 22:24–25, NKJV).

- "Ointment and perfume delight the heart, and the sweetness of a man's friend gives delight by hearty counsel" (Prov. 27:9, NKJV).

- "Do not forsake your own friend or your father's friend" (Prov. 27:10, NKJV).

What we learn from these verses is not to be friends with angry, bitter people. They'll get you in trouble. A good friend gives you good counsel and advice, and because she loves you, she's going to tell you the truth and what you need to know to live your best life. We also see that we should not leave or forsake our friends or our father's friends. This is wisdom speaking.

Getting back to our main verse, Proverbs 27:17, we learn that friends can sharpen us and help us get our edge back.

We've been talking about those times in life when the challenges seem harder than we think we can bear. We have been knocked down by illness, grief, unemployment, financial strain, or other circumstances that are sometimes out of our control. We feel beaten down, shut out, uninspired, discouraged, and even dulled by the hardship. The Amplified version of Ecclesiastes 10:10 says: "If the ax is dull and he does not sharpen its edge, then he must exert more strength; but wisdom [to sharpen the ax] helps him succeed [with less effort]." Sharpening the ax means you're able to do more with less. With a sharp ax, you're able to succeed, or accomplish more, with less effort.

HAVE YOU LOST YOUR SHARPNESS?

All of us are instruments in the hands of God, and sometimes we lose our sharpness. You can lose your sharpness in the prophetic. You can lose your sharpness in prayer. You can lose your sharpness in deliverance and discernment. You can lose your sharpness in life.

Have you ever seen someone and thought, "Wow, they don't look good. They're not dressing well anymore"? Maybe it's happened to you, and you say to yourself, "What happened? I used to be a sharp dresser. I used to have it all together. When did I start letting myself go?"

Well, even when we don't want to, sometimes we lose our edge. All of us at various times in life can become discouraged, tired, emotionally or spiritually weary, and frustrated. We lose our edge. Yet I am writing to you today to encourage you that God has a comeback planned for you.

When you lose your edge, don't throw in the towel and don't throw away the sword. Instead, sharpen it! You may have a set of knives in your kitchen dulled from use. Many times people just throw them away. They may not realize they can sharpen those knives. All they need is a knife sharpener to restore them. Chefs sharpen their knives and keep them for a lifetime. They invest in expensive knives and don't just throw them away.

Sometimes we throw people away because they've lost their edge. We just dispose of them. We may even throw ourselves away. We give up. But we need to know that God has invested in us. He bought us at a high price and has no intention of tossing us aside. He doesn't wish for any of us to perish. He wants to sharpen your edge so that you feel useful again.

IRON SHARPENS IRON

One of the ways you sharpen a knife's edge is by rubbing it against another sharp instrument—"iron sharpens iron"—or using what's called a sharpening stone. The more you use a sword or a knife, the duller it becomes. Sometimes in life you're working and exerting energy, you're laboring, and you're doing so much that you lose your edge.

You used to be sharp. Business, sharp. Decision making, sharp. The way you dressed, the way you looked, sharp. The way you spoke, sharp. Your prophetic gift, sharp. Discernment, sharp. But something happened and suddenly you got tired, weary, and frustrated. You lost your edge, and you're not doing as well as you used to.

I like what *The Preacher's Complete Homiletical Commentary on the Old Testament* says about this verse: "The sword that has seen much hard service must come in contact with another steel instrument to restore its edge."[1]

Have you been in a lot of battles? Have you been like a sword? When a warrior goes into a battle with a sword and he's fighting with that sword, the sword will lose its edge after a period of time. You are a spiritual warrior, and you have been in battles. You've been fighting. You've been using the sword of the Word of God, but you've lost your edge. It happens as we battle and fight.

Hear this again: "The sword that has seen much hard service must come in contact with another steel instrument to restore its edge. The ploughshare that has pushed its way through hard and stony ground must be fitted for more work by friction with a whetstone."[2]

Have you been plowing hard ground? After a while, that plow will become dull. It needs to be sharpened so it can cut through that hard and difficult terrain.

> The axe, after it has felled many trees, must be subjected to a similar process. So the intellectual and spiritual nature of man becomes at times in need of a stimulus from without which may fitly be compared with this sharpening of iron by iron.[3]

All of us need this. We all go through times of tiredness and weariness. We've been in battles. We've been cutting through hard ground. We've been cutting down a lot of trees. We've been using our faith and our spiritual instruments, and after a while they become dull.

> Hard mental toil, contact with uncongenial persons and things, disappointments, and even great spiritual emotions, have a tendency to exhaust our energies and depress our spirits, and render us for a time indisposed to exertion, and perhaps incapable of it.[4]

If you're exhausted, you may think or say things like, "I'm just tired. I can't cut down another tree. I can't fight another battle. I can't plow any more ground. I've lost my edge. I've lost my sharpness. It's too hard."

The worst thing you can do is give up. There's nothing wrong with you just because you're tired and weary. You just need to be sharpened. You're not defective. Don't throw yourself away. Get sharpened. You can still be used in business, in ministry, and in what God has called you to do.

I don't want you to feel condemned or guilty or give up in life because you lost your edge. At certain times all of us do. Some ministries have lost their edge; they're no longer on the cutting edge. Some have lost their edge in preaching, teaching, and prophesying. It's not that God has rejected them; it's that they've become dull.

But you, you must get your edge back. Preacher, you must get your edge back. Prophet, you must get your edge back. You used to be so accurate in the word of knowledge, and you used to have such a cutting-edge word. You were so accurate and so sharp in discernment, but you've lost it. Prayer warrior, intercessor, you must get your edge back. Businessperson, you must get your edge back. You must get your edge back, man or woman of God. Whoever you are—whatever gifting, anointing, talent, or role you have in the marketplace or in the kingdom and body of Christ—you must get your edge back.

Being sharp is so important. Whether it's your prayer ministry, your prophetic ministry, your business, or your finances, being sharp is a key to prosperity and fruitfulness. A woodsman was once asked,

"What would you do if you had just five minutes to chop down a tree?" He answered, "I would spend the first two and a half minutes sharpening my ax."[5]

Wow! That's wisdom. In other words, he wouldn't just start attacking the tree. No; he would spend half the time sharpening his ax because he knows that if the ax is sharp, it will take less time to cut down the tree. There's wisdom in sharpening the ax.

God wants to see you get your edge back and will cause the right people and situations to come into your life to sharpen you. I believe that as you read and pray through this chapter, the words I have written will minister to you. You are going to learn how to get back a sharp countenance and your edge.

THE RIGHT PEOPLE KEEP YOU SHARP

One of the wisest things you can do in life is to get with people who sharpen you. If you have lost your edge, get with people who can sharpen you. A friend, coach, mentor, pastor, or intercessor—these are some of the people who can help restore your edge. Do you have these people around you? Who is helping you get your edge back?

You're tired and weary. A look from a friend or a word of encouragement from a mentor can help you rekindle fresh hope and therefore new life for renewed action. It's important to have prophetic friends. It's important to have friends who pray and can sharpen your countenance.

When I read Proverbs 27:17, I asked, "God, what does this word *countenance* mean? How is a person's countenance sharpened?" I had to really dig deep into this scripture. The Easy-to-Read Version says, "As one piece of iron sharpens another, so friends keep each other sharp."

A true friend will keep you sharp and notice when you're losing your edge, when you don't have it together, and when you're falling away. A true friend will notice when you're dragging, down, and depressed, and when you no longer have the ability to get things done—and they'll tell you. A true friend will keep you sharp.

Lord, give us friends who keep us sharp!

Sometimes you've lost your edge and don't even know it, but your friend notices it and says so: "This is not you. You're better than this. You're sharper than this. You're more talented than this. You do better work than this. You dress better than this. You look better than this. You talk better than this. Your countenance is not sharp. I can see it in your face. I can see the way you look. You've lost your edge."

Do you have friends who talk to you like this? Friends who are honest with you and speak the truth directly and in love? Do you have friends who keep you sharp? Friends who will not just let you look like anything and live like anything? Friends who will notice when you're losing your image or keenness?

You want friends like this. When you've lost that X-factor or special sauce that made you distinct, they'll notice it and tell you. They'll help sharpen you and keep you sharp. Pray this now: "Lord, give me people who will keep me sharp."

A SHARP COUNTENANCE

The Bible makes a compelling point about this type of friendship: "As iron sharpens iron, so a man sharpens the countenance of his friend" (Prov. 27:17, NKJV). A friend knows your countenance. If you have a good countenance, your face is shiny and your skin glows. The glory of God and the joy of the Lord show on your face. But when you become depressed, tired, angry, and frustrated, your countenance changes.

You can try to fake it. You can smile, but a friend knows. A covenant friend says, "You're smiling, but you're not happy. You're smiling, but something is wrong. I can look at your countenance and tell you're not glowing."

You know what I mean. You have probably seen someone who just had a glow all around them. You may have even been compelled to say something about it: "Man, you look good," or "Girl, you are just glowing. You look happy, and it's just all over your face."

Other times, when someone isn't well for any number of reasons, you may say, "You don't look so good." The way we respond to a friend's face or the way they respond to ours leads us to understand that the word *countenance* is a reflection of whatever is happening inside you—as in your character, emotions, or mood. Your countenance is a reflection of your character, of what's inside.

The Scripture has a lot to say about our countenance. The word *countenance* is

> the translation of a variety of Hebrew and Greek expressions, *panim*; *prosopon*, being the most frequent. Besides these, there are *mar'eh*, "appearance," "shape," "comeliness," "visage," "ayin," "the eye," *to'ar*, "appearance," "figure," etc., and Aramaic *ziw*. To the Oriental the countenance mirrors, even more than to us, the character and feelings of the heart. The countenance (*mar'eh*) is "fair" (1 Sam. 17:42; 2 Sam. 14:27; Dan. 1:15); in 1 Sam. 16:12, literally, "fair of eyes"; "comely" (Song 2:14); "beautiful" ([~*to'ar*, 1 Sam. 25:3); "cheerful" (*panim*, Prov. 15:13); "angry" (Prov. 15:23); "fierce" (Dan. 8:23); "troubled" (Ezek. 27:35); "sad" (1 Sam. 1:18; Neh. 2:2, 3; Eccl. 7:3). The countenance is "sharpened" i.e. made keen (Prov. 27:17); it "falls," i.e. looks despondent, disappointed (Gen. 4:5, 6); is "cast down" (Job 29:24); "changed" (Job 14:20; compare "altered" into glory, Lk. 9:29; Dan. 5:6, 9, 10; 7:28, Aramaic *ziw*).[6]

God also has a countenance, a face. One of God's blessings is found in Psalm 4:6: "Lord, lift thou up the light of thy countenance upon us." In this verse we can see that countenance can be a picture of something glorious. So maybe we can understand why countenance is important and why God wants your countenance, your face, sharpened. It is a reflection of your inward parts. God uses people to sharpen your countenance.

When you lose your edge, you become tired. You become despondent, depressed, sorrowful, and sad. You lose the joy of the Lord. Your whole countenance changes. You no longer have that zeal, that fire, that light in your eyes, and that joy and excitement on your face. Work becomes hard. Ministry, business, and living become hard because you've lost your edge.

THE SHARPENING EDGE OF A COVENANT FRIEND

A covenant friend can sharpen your countenance. She can release a word of encouragement that tells you, "Look, get it together. You're not going out like this. You're too talented. You're too anointed. You have too much in you; too many people are depending on you. God loves you. God is with you. God has called you. God has sent you. Come on, get up and wash your face. Change your clothes. Let's go out. Let's go have lunch. Let's go have dinner. You're not going to lie around here depressed and looking sad, weary, and tired. No, you're going to get your edge back."

If I can be a friend who sharpens you from afar today, I have a word for you too. God says, "You're going to get your edge back. I'm going to cause your friends to sharpen you."

Now, if you don't have any friends, I pray that God would put in your life a prophetic person who's pulling for you, who wants to sharpen and help you, to encourage you and build you up. I declare that when this person speaks to you, his words will sharpen your countenance and get your gift moving again. Let his words sharpen your ministry, business, and finances.

If you've been depressed and discouraged, you've lost the joy in the glory of God in your face. If you're dragging your way to work and you're barely making it—if you look like you've been run over by the ugly train and your countenance is dry, empty, and gray—let the beauty of God come and light up your countenance. Let your sword be sharpened. Let your life get back on the cutting edge. Let iron sharpen iron. Let God put someone in your life who will always keep you sharp.

I feel the anointing on this so strong. I feel the glory of God as I write these words. You are receiving a new encouragement and a new sharpness. A new ability is coming back to your life. God is about to sharpen your countenance. He is going to give you people who love you and will keep you sharp. They will give you those words that will bring you the teaching and the correction you need to get back on track.

This goes for me too. I don't plan, as I get older

in ministry, to lose my sharpness in the prophetic in preaching and teaching. I'm going to keep myself sharp. I'm going to hang around people who help sharpen me. I'm going to get around prophets and apostles, coaches and mentors, and other believers who will help sharpen me. They will keep my countenance sharpened so I will not grow old, grumpy, mean, ugly, tired, worn out, and dull. No, that is not the will of God. God wants me to keep my edge sharpened.

FASTING SHARPENS YOUR EDGE

God is going to do something in your life. He is going to give you wisdom concerning what you need to get your edge back. We've already discovered the role that friends, mentors, pastors, intercessors, and coaches play in helping us get our edge back, but there's more we can do.

Sometimes fasting helps us get our sharpness and discernment back. You may consider doing what I call a "momentum fast" to get your momentum back or to keep it up. There are seasons in life, especially like the one many of us around the world saw in 2020, that cause us to lose momentum. The circumstances pile on and seem to take the wind out of our sails. But I declare that you will not lose your edge. You will finish out the season—whatever you are facing—with your momentum intact. Continue to believe the word of the Lord, and you will be established; believe His prophets, and you will prosper.

You can prosper when it looks like everything's going down. Prosperity is not based on how the economy looks or what the unemployment figures are. God is your God. He is Jehovah Jireh. He is your shalom. He is your prosperity. He is more than enough. Sometimes you need to fast to be able to reset your focus and to reset your eyes on God. You need to fast to once again be able to incline your ear to God and hear again what He has said and what He has promised—and faith comes by hearing.

MAY YOU BECOME THE SHARPENING STONE

As iron sharpens your iron, you are going to become like a sharpening stone. You're going to be the sharpening stone to sharpen others in your path. You're going to be like iron. As you get your edge back, you will come into contact with people who have lost their edge, and *you're* going to sharpen them. When people connect with you—if you're a coach, mentor, pastor, or friend—God is going to use you as a sharpening stone, a whetstone. We saw this word earlier in the chapter—a whetstone is a sharpening stone.

Just as a chef uses the whetstone to sharpen his expensive knives to restore them to their original value, you will also become a very valuable instrument again. Just because you've lost your edge does not mean you've lost your value. Maybe someone has told you you're no longer valuable, but you still are. You have a gift that is valuable. Your talent is still valuable. God is not throwing you away. What He put in you is still valuable. A person may try to throw you away, but God never would. He's going to restore your sharpness until you are like a whetstone. Believe me when I say that God is going to use your life, your church, your ministry, your business—whatever your ability is—as a sharpening stone.

WHERE THERE'S FRICTION, THERE'S HEAT

Sometimes the sharpening process is not pleasant. When you hit two pieces of iron together, sparks are produced and heat is emitted. This friction causes the blade to become sharp. You may have gone through some things. It's been tough. It's been hot. But God is saying, "I'm using that to sharpen you."

When you come out of that trial or those tests the enemy sent to destroy you, instead of the trial destroying you, God is going to use that adversity to sharpen you. A friend's rebuke or correction is much like friction created through iron sharpening iron. It may not be pleasant, and it may not feel good to your flesh, but it is just what you need to be made sharp again.

Let God sharpen you. Let Him sharpen your gift and talent. Let Him sharpen your countenance. Iron sharpens iron. Wood doesn't sharpen iron. It takes another strong piece of metal to sharpen iron. You need some strong people in your life—strong friends, strong apostles and prophets. Because you're a strong instrument—in your character and gifting—you need another strong instrument to help you maintain or restore your use and value. Iron sharpens iron.

Don't run away from strong relationships and strong friendships. Don't run away from iron and the sharpening process. It's the only thing that will shift and move you up in life.

PRAYER FOR GETTING BACK ON THE CUTTING EDGE

Lord, I pray I'll get my edge back and that my countenance will be sharpened. I pray that I get my edge back in business and ministry. I pray that my sword, my ax, my threshing instrument will be sharpened—that through me God will thresh the mountains and cut down the obstacles. I pray that I become the ax that will be laid to the root of the tree. May my ax become so sharp that it quickly cuts down every tree that I have not been able to cut down and uproot from my life.

I pray that my gift will become so sharp that what took me years and so much strength to do as I grew tired and weary, I will do in less time and with less strength. I pray that I will work smarter and not harder because my ax is sharp, my gift is sharp, my knowledge is sharp, my wisdom and understanding are sharp, and my skills are sharp.

Lord, sharpen me in Your Word. Sharpen me so that I am able to cut through the works of darkness—through witchcraft, sorcery, divination, and wickedness.

Make me sharp again, O God. Make me a sharp instrument, a sharpening stone: a whetstone. Let anyone who comes around me become sharper. Let me sharpen my friends.

PRAYER FOR A SHARP COUNTENANCE

Father, I thank You for this word of wisdom, this key of wisdom that You released to me today. I prophesy and decree that I am getting my edge back. I am getting my countenance back. The glory of God is coming back to my face. The joy of the Lord is coming back to my face. The fire of God is coming back to my eyes. My face will not be downcast and depressed. My countenance will not be angry, sad, or defeated. My head is lifted up. My countenance, my inward part—my character—will be sharpened. The glow, the glory, the light, the splendor, the beauty, and the cleanliness of the Lord are going to come back to my face.

Thank You, Father, for sharpening my countenance. Let Your glory bring back the light in my eyes. Let the smile and glory of God come back. Let the light of Your countenance shine upon my face.

Lord, give me a makeover so that joy and gladness can be seen on my face. Let victory be in my face. Let it be in my eyes. Sharpen my vision. Give me the eyes of an eagle. Give me keen insight. Give me keen discernment. Let me peer into the future. Let me see into the distance. Let me have pinpoint accuracy. Let me be able to focus in on the smallest details. Let me see what others miss. Let me get around people who have sharp vision. Let me have friends who have sharp discernment. Let iron sharpen iron.

PRAYER FOR GOOD FRIENDS

Lord, I pray that You will give me good friends who will love me and sharpen me. Give me friends who will sharpen my countenance; friends who will lift me up; friends who will help me; friends who will not let me slide, go backward, or go down. Lord, let me have friends who will not let me stay in a low place.

Lord, I pray for divine, supernatural friends. Give me new friends and remove those who have betrayed me or left me in my time of need.

I pray that You would give me two friends: a covenant friend—a friend that sticks closer than a brother—and a friend who will sharpen me.

I pray that You will give me strong friends, prophetic friends, intercessory friends, prayer warrior friends, friends who help encourage and build me, and friends who will give me revelation. Lord, give me friends who will tell me I can make it, friends who will stir me up and impart to me, and friends who will give me good counsel. I pray that their iron would sharpen my iron. In Jesus' name, I pray. Amen.

CHAPTER 11

KEEP DREAMING

> *Even Joseph, who was sold for a servant: whose feet they hurt with fetters: he was laid in iron: until the time that his word came: the word of the L*ORD *tried him.*
>
> —P SALM 105:17–19

JOSEPH'S GIFT OF dream interpretation was one of the things that caused him to prosper and rise to the place where God intended for him to go. Joseph was the victim of envy, hatred, and jealousy from his brothers. They even tried to kill him, but he was spared. He was the victim of lies. His integrity was attacked to the point that he found himself in prison. Yet Joseph was a good steward and a good servant. He served his master faithfully. He was honest. He was a man of integrity. He was good-looking, which got him in trouble with Potiphar's wife.

Joseph was approximately seventeen years old when he was taken into Egypt by the company of Ishmaelites on their way to Egypt. (See Genesis 37:23–36.) So he was a teenager when he ended up in Potiphar's house. After being falsely accused of raping Potiphar's wife, Joseph spent about ten years in prison. By the time he stood before Pharaoh, interpreted his dream, and was promoted to second in command of all of Egypt, Joseph was thirty years old. Talk about time and process. Talk about deferred hope and delayed justice. Can you wait thirteen years for vindication? Can you wait thirteen years for your hopes and dreams to manifest? Can you endure the lies, betrayal, wrongful imprisonment, and judgment while you wait?

You may be in a season now where it feels like whatever could go wrong has or will; can you wait for the vengeance of God? Can you dare to trust and believe His prophets and the word of the Lord that was spoken about your approaching time of greatness, prosperity, and promotion? I pray that you can and that you stay built up in faith until the appointed time comes.

There are so many lessons we can learn from the life of Joseph. I believe God put his story in Scripture so that we can benefit from it.

IS THE WORD OF THE LORD TRYING YOU?

Imagine spending thirteen years of your life in a place of obscurity, a place away from your family. Joseph probably spent about three years in Potiphar's house and about ten years in prison. Now, I believe that it was during this time that God was working to form in Joseph some important attributes. He had the word of the Lord. He had a prophetic dream. He knew what God had said, but that word was trying him.

The Scripture says, "Even Joseph, who was sold for a servant: whose feet they hurt with fetters: he was laid in iron: until the time that his word came: the word of the LORD tried him" (Ps. 105:17–19). What does that mean? It means you can have a prophetic dream, you can have a prophetic word, and it can look like everything is going in the opposite direction. God showed Joseph that he would have dominion over his brothers. But it looked like there was no way he could possibly see the fulfillment of that dream while he was away from his family in Egypt, in Potiphar's house, and then in prison. Still, he had a choice: he could hold on to that dream and believe God, or he could give in to doubt and unbelief and stop dreaming altogether.

The word of the Lord will test and try you to see whether or not you really believe, because we walk by faith and not by sight. It may start out looking like everything is going in the opposite direction of your dream or your vision—what God has shown you for your ministry, your life, your family, your children, and your business. But God has given you a prophetic dream. He has given you a prophetic word. And as that word tests you, you have to choose how you will stand up to the test: Will you believe God? Will you hold on to His prophetic word for you? Will you walk by faith and not by sight? Will you believe? Will you not stagger at His promise? Will you give up? Will you become discouraged? Will you hold on and believe that dream, that vision, that prophetic word, in spite of the way it looks? That's how God's word tries us.

So Joseph was in prison. He was put in a place with the king's prisoners. Because he was there, he came into contact with two prisoners: Pharaoh's butler and Pharaoh's baker. One day he saw they were sad and asked them, "Why are you so sad? Why has your countenance fallen?" (See Genesis 40:6–7.) And they told him, "We have dreamed a dream, and there is no interpreter of it." Joseph responded, "Do not interpretations belong to God? Tell me them, I pray you" (v. 8).

Now we see Joseph's gift manifesting. Joseph was a dreamer. He also had a gift of interpreting dreams. His gift was his ticket out of prison. Likewise, your gift is very important because your gift can actually cause you to come out of a bad situation. Your gift can cause you to be promoted and exalted.

The butler told his dream first. It was about a vine, three clusters of grapes being crushed and put into a cup. Joseph told him that in three days he was going to be restored to his position as butler. Then Joseph said, "But remember me when it is well with you, and please show kindness to me; make mention of me to Pharaoh, and get me out of this house: For indeed I was stolen away from the land of the Hebrews; and also I have done nothing here that they should put me into the dungeon" (vv. 14–15, NKJV). In other words Joseph told him, "Don't forget about me."

Then when the baker heard the interpretation of the butler's dream, he told Joseph his dream. But it was not favorable. "Within three days," Joseph told him, "Pharaoh will lift off your head from you and hang you on a tree; and the birds will eat your flesh from you" (v. 19, NKJV).

Everything happened just as Joseph said it would. The butler was released and put back into his position in Pharaoh's court, and the baker was hanged. But the butler forgot all about Joseph. He did not remember him.

Asking the butler to remember him was Joseph's attempt to get out of prison. Joseph knew it was not the place he was destined to be. It was not part of his prophetic word or his prophetic dream to be in a dungeon. The dungeon was the opposite of a place of dominion and authority where his family would actually have to submit to him. So he was trying his best to find a way out. The butler could have gone and entreated for Joseph and demanded his release. Instead, he forgot him. This is another hurtful thing that happened to Joseph. Joseph was forgotten.

YOU ARE NOT FORGOTTEN

What do you do when people forget you and your plight? Like Pharaoh's butler, they can be blessed by you and then walk away from you, forgetting the blessing you put into their lives. Ministers deal with this all the time. They can be great blessings to people, and those same people will walk away and forget all about them as if they had never been a part of their lives. Joseph felt forsaken. The Scriptures don't specify how long he had to sit in that prison wondering what happened to the butler after he was restored.

The good news is that God did not forget about Joseph. This is what I love about this story. Even though people will forget you, *God will never forget you*. He'll never forsake you. God knew exactly where Joseph was. He knew exactly the timing and the season. He knew that Pharaoh was about to have a dream and the butler would remember and even say, "I've not done right. There was a young man who interpreted my dream, and I forgot about him" (Gen. 41:9–13, author's paraphrase).

I don't know if the butler was so happy when he got out and was restored to his family and position that he just forgot about Joseph. Maybe there was a welcoming ceremony and he got so caught up in being restored that Joseph's circumstances completely left his mind. But on that day in Pharaoh's chambers he remembered the young man who had interpreted his dream.

NEVER STOP BLESSING PEOPLE

Joseph came out of prison because of his gift of dream interpretation. He interpreted not only Pharaoh's dream but also the butler's and the baker's while he was in prison. Notice that Joseph's gift worked in the lowest place, a place that did not seem conducive to using it. Your gift will work anywhere. That's why I love the gifts of God. The Bible says, "Stir up the gift of God, which is in you" (2 Tim. 1:6, NKJV). Don't neglect the gift of God. Never shut down your gift, even when it looks like you belong in another place. Your gift can work anywhere people are, wherever there's a need. It may not be the biggest platform. It may not be the largest church. It may not be the best place. It may be in the dungeon, as it was for Joseph. But because of his interpretation of the butler's (and baker's) dream, Joseph's gift was the exit ramp for his release from prison. He willingly moved in his gift in a less-than-ideal place.

Joseph was a dreamer. He interpreted dreams. You may be a dreamer too. Maybe you simply dream, or maybe you also interpret dreams. You may be one who prophesies, preaches, or teaches. You may be one who has a gift in business. You have power to get wealth. You may have any number of other graces operating in your life. Yet you sometimes find yourself in a place that seems opposite of where you should be based on your dream, your vision, or a prophetic word. This was true in Joseph's life. He found himself in prison, in a dungeon, yet he didn't pout or get angry and bitter. Joseph remained open and willing to help others. "Tell me your dream," he said.

No matter where you find yourself along the journey to seeing your dream fulfilled, always let your gift bless someone else. Serving others is the key to promotion, prosperity, and elevation. Never allow yourself to become so frustrated by the way things look that you stop blessing people. Keep blessing others. God will eventually cause you to be blessed. You shall recover all.

YOU *WILL* COME OUT OF THIS

Yes, Joseph did eventually come out of prison, and you too will come out of whatever dungeon you're in. Can you imagine what Joseph must have felt when he got the call? Out of nowhere he learned that Pharaoh wanted to see him. Suddenly he was standing before Pharaoh, interpreting his dream. Suddenly a ring was put on his finger and a royal garment was placed upon his shoulders. Why? Because in the lowest place in the dungeon, Joseph still let his gift operate. He helped someone. He blessed someone. He interpreted a dream.

Are you willing to help bless other people even while you're in a low or obscure place—a place where no one sees you? A prison represents obscurity. Show me a man or woman of God who has any level of prominence, and I guarantee you there was a time when he or she was hidden—forgotten. There was a time he had to preach to small numbers of people. She had to preach in living rooms or basements, small churches or storefronts, to ten or twenty people. He preached in places where no one knew him. She preached when no one listened to her and no one invited her to their platform. But this person was faithful to use his or her gifts. He or she was faithful to be a blessing in a place of obscurity.

It's in the places of obscurity that God develops us and grows our faith. He builds our character and patience. He uses our dreams and visions to test and try us. Are you in it just for the dream?

When he was seventeen, Joseph dreamed of his rise to leadership. It was thirteen years later that those early dreams began to manifest themselves. The vision, the prophetic word will try us. We have to hold on to it. We have to believe God for it in spite of the way it looks. Because the dream is from God, it will come to pass—*if* you maintain your integrity, walk in righteousness, demonstrate character, do not forsake the dream, and do not give up on your destiny and your future. It will come to pass even though it may seem as if it's delayed.

AGAIN I SAY, "DON'T GIVE UP"

Don't give up. This is the tremendous lesson we learn from the life of Joseph. Don't give up on your dream.

Don't give up on your vision. Don't give up on the prophetic word that God has given you. Suddenly Joseph came out of prison after years of being mistreated and lied about and living in obscurity. Suddenly Joseph was promoted to a place of authority because he blessed someone in the obscure place. God had a time and a season prepared when Joseph's character was sturdy to bring him out of that particular prison.

As we close this time together, I'm praying that if you have a dream, a vision, a prophetic word, a destiny from God, that God would cause you—even in your season when it looks like the dream is not coming to pass—to operate in your gift and your calling, and that you do what you have been graced to do despite the circumstances you're facing. I'm praying that God will cause that long-held dream to manifest suddenly. I decree the "suddenlies" of God. I speak suddenlies to happen and manifest in your life this year and in the future. I decree that whatever you've lost will be recovered sevenfold and return in greater measure than you had before. You shall recover all.

Would you pray this prayer with me now?

PRAYER TO RECOVER ALL AND SEE THE FULFILLMENT OF YOUR DREAMS

Father, thank You for the lessons, revelations, and insights You made available from the life of

Joseph. Thank You, Father, for his example. I thank You that my gift will operate in that place of obscurity, the low place—a dungeon and a prison. Lord, I pray that the dream and vision You've given me will manifest and come to pass. May I receive "suddenly." May You promote me and cause my dream to manifest. I pray, Lord, that You would give me the strength to hold on to my dream, to confess it, and to wait patiently for it to manifest.

Lord, give me the endurance to not give up on my dream and not lose hope. Let me be encouraged today. I decree favor as it was on Joseph. Let the gift of God that dwells within me be stirred. Let me not neglect the gift of God operating in me, even if I am called to use it in a small or obscure place.

I will not walk away from my calling, destiny, and purpose. I will not give up on it. I will not go back into sin. I will not leave You, God. I will not depart from the things You have shown me.

I will be encouraged and know that even though people may forget about me, even though it may look as if I am suffering from a season of loneliness and discouragement and that I am all by myself in an obscure place, You have not forgotten me. You are with me. As You were with Joseph in that prison, that obscure place, You will be with me. Just as You gave Joseph favor in that obscure place, You will give me favor in that obscure place. Your presence, O God, will cause me to prosper.

Even if people put me in a low place, no weapon formed against me shall prosper. Every tongue that comes against me shall fall. God, You will cause me to triumph over my enemies; over envy, jealousy, hatred, murder, lies, and deception. Whatever tries to come against me to sabotage the dream You have given me, I decree that it will not prosper. I pray this over my life today. In Jesus' name, amen.

NOTES

CHAPTER 1

1. "Louisiana Residents Dig Out From Two Hurricanes in Six Weeks," CNBC, October 11, 2020, https://www.cnbc.com/2020/10/11/louisiana-residents-dig-out-from-two-hurricanes-in-six-weeks.html; Duke Carter, "Louisiana Food Banks Turn From One Crisis to Another as Laura Recovery Begins," WWLTV, August 30, 2020, https://www.wwltv.com/article/weather/severe-weather/louisiana-food-banks-turns-from-one-crisis-to-another-as-laura-recovery-begins/289-bb53b548-9c2b-49d9-ae59-d137a0dc6bbd.

CHAPTER 3

1. "George Floyd: What Happened in the Final Moments of His Life," BBC News, July 16, 2020, https://www.bbc.com/news/world-us-canada-52861726.

2. "The True Death Toll of COVID-19: Estimating Global Excess Mortality," World Health Organization, accessed October 15, 2021, https://www.who.int/data/stories/

the-true-death-toll-of-covid-19-estimating-global-excess-mortality.

CHAPTER 5

1. "Healing Trauma With Our Dreams," National Institute for the Clinical Application of Behavioral Medicine, accessed September 16, 2021, https://www.nicabm.com/sleep-dream/.

2. Charity Kayembe, "Dream Declarations and Activation: Prayer of Activation," Glory Waves, accessed September 16, 2021, https://www.glorywaves.org/dream-declarations-activation/. Used and adapted by permission.

CHAPTER 6

1. *Merriam-Webster*, s.v. "capacity," accessed September 16, 2021, https://www.merriam-webster.com/dictionary/capacity.

2. *Merriam-Webster*, s.v. "large," accessed September 16, 2021, https://www.merriam-webster.com/dictionary/large.

3. Blue Letter Bible, s.v. "*leb*," accessed September 16, 2021, https://www.blueletterbible.org/lexicon/h3820/kjv/wlc/0-1/.

CHAPTER 7

1. *Merriam-Webster*, s.v. "shame," accessed September 16, 2021, https://www.merriam-webster.com/dictionary/shame.

2. Google Dictionary, s.v. "shame," accessed September 16, 2021, https://www.google.com/search?client=firefox-b-1-d&q=google+dictionary#dobs=shame.

CHAPTER 8

1. Blue Letter Bible, s.v. "*eres*," accessed September 16, 2021, https://www.blueletterbible.org/lexicon/h776/kjv/wlc/0-1/.

CHAPTER 10

1. *The Preacher's Complete Homiletical Commentary on the Old Testament*, vol. 13 (New York: Funk & Wagnalls, 1892), 734.

2. *The Preacher's Complete Homiletical Commentary on the Old Testament*, 734.

3. *The Preacher's Complete Homiletical Commentary on the Old Testament*, 734.

4. *The Preacher's Complete Homiletical Commentary on the Old Testament*, 734.

5. Quote Investigator, s.v. "woodsman," accessed September 16, 2021, https://quoteinvestigator.com/tag/woodsman/.
6. NET Bible, s.v. "countenance," accessed September 16, 2021, http://classic.net.bible.org/dictionary.php?word=Countenance.

www.ingramcontent.com/pod-product-compliance
Lightning Source LLC
Chambersburg PA
CBHW010044090426
42735CB00018B/3386